BEST
LOVED
BERNARD
SHAW

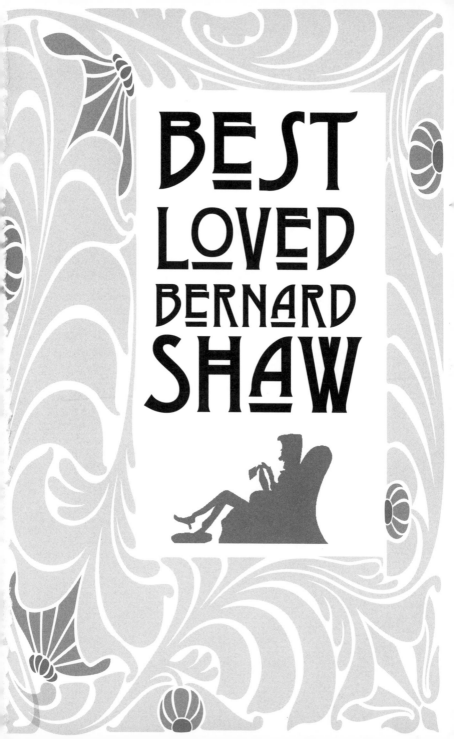

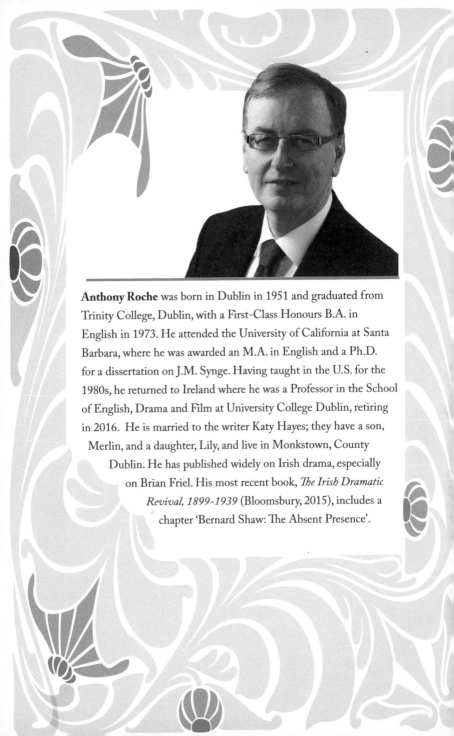

Anthony Roche was born in Dublin in 1951 and graduated from Trinity College, Dublin, with a First-Class Honours B.A. in English in 1973. He attended the University of California at Santa Barbara, where he was awarded an M.A. in English and a Ph.D. for a dissertation on J.M. Synge. Having taught in the U.S. for the 1980s, he returned to Ireland where he was a Professor in the School of English, Drama and Film at University College Dublin, retiring in 2016. He is married to the writer Katy Hayes; they have a son, Merlin, and a daughter, Lily, and live in Monkstown, County Dublin. He has published widely on Irish drama, especially on Brian Friel. His most recent book, *The Irish Dramatic Revival, 1899-1939* (Bloomsbury, 2015), includes a chapter 'Bernard Shaw: The Absent Presence'.

BEST
LOVED
BERNARD
SHAW

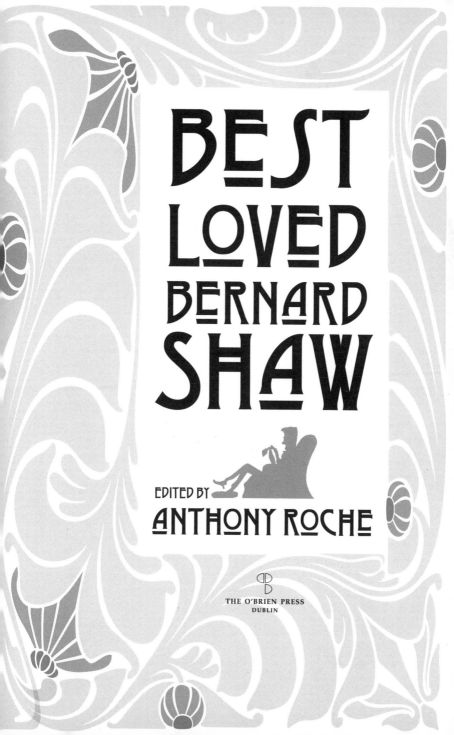

EDITED BY
ANTHONY ROCHE

THE O'BRIEN PRESS
DUBLIN

First published 2021 by The O'Brien Press Ltd.
12 Terenure Road East, Rathgar, Dublin 6, D06 HD27, Ireland.
Tel: +353 1 4923333; Fax: +353 1 4922777
E-mail: books@obrien.ie; Website: www.obrien.ie
The O'Brien Press is a member of Publishing Ireland.

ISBN: 978-1-78849-053-5

1 2 3 4 5
21 22 23 24 25

Cover illustration: Emma Byrne
Editing, typesetting, layout and design: The O'Brien Press Ltd
Printed and bound in Poland by Białostockie Zakłady Graficzne S.A.

The paper in this book is produced using pulp from managed forests.

Every effort has been made to trace copyright holders and to obtain their permission
for the use of copyright material. The publisher apologises for any errors or omissions
and would be grateful if notified of any corrections that should be incorporated in future
reprints or editions of this book.

All photos courtesy of Alamy with the exception of p110, Siobhán McKenna,
permission granted by Barry Houlihan, Archivist, NUI Galway.

Published in
DUBLIN
UNESCO
City of Literature

To Peter Gahan and Nelson O'Ceallaigh Ritschel

CONTENTS

INTRODUCTION   page 9

CHAPTER ONE: SOCIALISM   19

  'A Manifesto' (Fabian Tracts no. 2)   22

  Lecture on Socialism   25

  From *The Intelligent Woman's Guide to*   28
    Socialism and Capitalism

CHAPTER TWO: IDEALISM AND REALISM   35

  The Prose and Plays of the 1890s   36

  From *The Quintessence of Ibsenism*   37

  From *Arms and the Man*   42

  From *Mrs. Warren's Profession*   47

CHAPTER THREE: THE NEW CENTURY AND A VISIONARY
THEATRE   53

  From *Man and Superman*   57

  From *John Bull's Other Island*   65

  From *Major Barbara*   69

CHAPTER FOUR: FLOWER GIRLS AND DUCHESSES 53

From *Pygmalion* 78

CHAPTER FIVE: THE FIRST WORLD WAR AND EASTER 1916 85

From *Common Sense About the War* 88

From *O'Flaherty V.C.* 92

From *Heartbreak House* 97

From 'A Discarded Defence of Roger Casement' 101

CHAPTER SIX: LATE SHAW 105

From *St. Joan* 107

From *The Millionairess* 114

From *Geneva* 120

CODA 124

SOURCES 126

ACKNOWLEDGEMENTS 128

Bernard Shaw: mens sana in corpore sano (a healthy mind in a healthy body); swimming in Cap d'Antibes at the age of ninety-three.

INTRODUCTION

George Bernard Shaw was one in a line of Irish writers who, from the close of the seventeenth century, emigrated to London at an early age and contributed plays to the repertory that are still staged: Goldsmith's *She Stoops to Conquer* (1773) for example, or Sheridan's *The School for Scandal* (1777). The two greatest examplars of this tradition emerged in the last decade of the nineteenth century, when Oscar Wilde (b. 1854) and Bernard Shaw (b. 1856) wrote a succession of comic masterpieces for the London stage.

Thereafter, their fates contrast markedly. Wilde achieved his greatest success with *The Importance of Being Earnest* (1895); by the end of that same year, he was in prison, dying in 1900 at the age of forty-six. Shaw continued unabated into the twentieth century; he rose to writing his most ambitious and challenging plays in the new century and lived in reasonably good health until 1950, dying at the age of ninety-four. He was by far the longest-lived and most productive of all of these playwrights, and the only one who made a decent and regular living from his writings.

Shaw started from the most unpropitious of beginnings. But he possessed a steely self-determination, and turned the unshakeable conviction that he would become a great writer into a self-fulfilling prophecy.

George Bernard Shaw was born in Dublin on 26 July 1856 to George Carr Shaw and Lucinda Elizabeth Gurley, who was known as Bessie. He had two older sisters, on whom his mother doted. The Shaws had aristocratic antecedents, but the family was in a sharp decline during his father's lifetime, to the degree that GBS termed himself a 'downstart'. George Carr Shaw held (and lost) a succession of office jobs and was finally taken in by his brother to work as a corn merchant.

Any display of feeling was frowned upon in this socially Protestant household, so Shaw learned to hide his emotions at an early age. His father was an alcoholic; Shaw became a lifelong teetotaller. (The vegetarianism came later, after reading Shelley.) But he enjoyed the way his father could laugh at his misfortunes and indulge in excruciating puns; Shaw's unfailing sense of humour came from George Carr Shaw. Bessie was serious and the artistic one; she loved music and bequeathed that lifelong passion to her son.

In the 1860s, an extraordinary change struck the Shaw household with the arrival of one George Vandaleur Lee.

A dedicated musician, he made Bessie Shaw his second-in-command, and then took the arrangement one step further by moving into the Shaw household and setting up his music school in their living room. Lee looked like Svengali and had a mesmerising turn of speech; it seems at least possible he was GBS's natural father.

Shaw hated inner-city Dublin, its squalor and foul-mouthed denizens. When Lee rented a summer cottage in Dalkey, Shaw discovered a beautiful landscape in which his imagination could wander and develop – the combination of realism and romance in his writings derives from his native place.

Lee upped anchor in 1873 and moved suddenly to London, and Bessie and the two Shaw girls followed in the same week. Three years later, at the age of nineteen, Shaw took the opportunity of attending his sister Yuppy's funeral (she died of tuberculosis at twenty-one) to move to London also and not return. Years later, he gave his reason: 'London was the literary centre for the English language, and for such artistic culture as the realm of the English language (in which I proposed to be king) could afford.'

That literary success by no means came quickly. For five successive years, Shaw wrote five novels, each of which was rejected in turn. The first money he earned from writing came from reviewing classical concerts under the psuedonym of Corno di Bassetto, turning his lifelong knowledge of music to practical account. That love of music was also to inform his writing of plays – a sequence like 'Don Juan in Hell' from *Man and Superman* (1901–3) makes more sense in terms of opera than the standard realism of the day.

Shaw also became a drama critic. If his musical advocacy was inspired by Wagner, in the theatre he promoted the dramatic innovations of Henrik Ibsen, currently scandalising Europe with plays like *A Doll's House* (1889) and *Ghosts* (1891).

In 1892, Shaw's first play, *Widower's Houses*, was staged. Co-written with Ibsen's English translator, William Archer, it was staged by JT Grein's Independent Theatre in London, where *Ghosts* had been performed the year before. Shaw's first play was only accorded two performances and was indifferently received. But it drew an enthusiastic response from his fellow playwright and Dubliner Oscar Wilde, who praised 'the horrible flesh and blood of your creatures'.

Wilde consciously paired himself with Shaw, dubbing them the 'great Celtic School' of dramatists. Shaw rose to Wilde's challenge, matching the former's succession of brilliant plays in the 1890s. They both created sharp-edged, witty comedies, either designed to challenge the censor or to reform the London stage. Shaw's plays were informed by an ever-deepening commitment to socialism, which he also pursued on the public platform as a lecturer.

In June 1898, Shaw married an Anglo-Irish heiress, Charlotte Payne-Townshend. She was independently wealthy but, lest it be thought he was fortune-hunting, Shaw pointed out that his plays were now earning him a good living, both through publication and production. Charlotte drew Shaw back to Ireland, thirty years after he had left it; several of his plays (*Major Barbara*, *Saint Joan*) were largely written there.

Yeats and Lady Gregory commissioned a play about Ireland from Shaw for the new Abbey Theatre; but *John Bull's Other Island* (1904) was not staged there until 1916. When the Lord Chamberlain's Reader banned Shaw's one-act play *The Shewing-Up of Blanco Posnet* for blasphemy, it was staged at the Abbey to great success in 1909.

Shaw continued to intervene at the Abbey over the years, defending Sean O'Casey's *The Silver Tassie* after the Abbey turned it down in 1928. But Shaw's theatrical career was mainly pursued in England, where he laid the foundations for a political theatre of ideas that was carried on later in the twentieth century by such writers as John Osborne and David Hare. When the Abbey turned down *John Bull*, the Royal Court Theatre in London was waiting and his Irish play was staged there to great success. The actor-dramatist Harley Granville-Barker and Shaw made a formidable team.

With the addition of Charlotte's income, Shaw was able to give up journalism. He could now devote himself to writing more ambitious and visionary plays, which the avant-garde theatrics and committed ensemble acting of the Royal Court were poised to stage.

Shaw and Charlotte were happily married for forty-four years (she predeceased him in 1943), but had no children. Their marriage was rumoured to be celibate, something Shaw did not deny. His more passionate and romantic side came out in a series of affairs with leading actresses, from Florence Farr and Ellen Terry through to Molly Tompkins in the 1940s. These romances were mostly conducted across the footlights, by letter and theatre review, but occasionally they were carried out face to face.

The most passionately engaged was with Mrs Patrick Campbell, the only one to seriously rattle Charlotte. Shaw had pitched upon Mrs Pat to play his cockney flower-seller in *Pygmalion* (1914). Eliza was nineteen; the actress forty-eight, but still radiant. Shaw and Mrs Pat eventually elected to meet at a seaside hotel, but she delayed and then funked their meeting. Shaw sent her an enormously wounded letter. John O'Donovan has shewdly pointed out that this was the same year (1913) in which Shaw's mother Bessie died, and that he badly needed consoling. Shaw and Mrs Pat remained friends, and she went on to triumph as Eliza.

Shaw's fortunes took a dive during the First World War, when he opposed the jingoistic patriotism of British involvement. His defense of Sir Roger Casement as an Irishman defending his country rather than an English traitor did not go over well either. But he won back favour with the huge success of *St Joan* in 1923, and was awarded the Nobel Prize for Literature in 1925. Shaw also made a successful transition into screenwriting, winning an Oscar for the script of *Pygmalion* in 1938.

The later Shaw proved less flexible in his thinking and showed a distressing tendency to cuddle up to dictators; he may have lived too long. In his will, he divided his estate into three equal portions: to train drama students at the Royal Academy of Dramatic Art; to the British Museum, whose Reading Room became his own private university when he first arrived in London (Shaw had left school at fifteen); and to the National Gallery of Ireland, whose paintings he had studied in detail when he first thought of becoming an artist.

Shaw said towards the end of his life that being born and raised an Irishman made him 'a foreigner in every other country. But the position of a foreigner with complete command of the same language has great advantages. I can take an objective view of England, which no Englishman can.'

Shaw addresses an audience in Portsmouth on socialism in 1910.

SOCIALISM

Bernard Shaw was a socialist all his life. The pamphlet 'A Manifesto' was published anonymously by the Fabian Society, a middle-class socialist organisation that worked for the betterment of society not through street protest but through articles, books and lectures. This approach eminently suited Shaw. Even when he had gained a name for himself, his numerous contributions on socialism to *The New Statesman* were frequently unsigned, because he was tired of playing the role of licensed court jester and wanted his arguments to be taken seriously. The editors were appalled, however, since the name of Shaw significantly increased sales.

The second extract is from a lecture Shaw gave in 1911 in North Staffordshire, the heart of the British industrial midlands. It is reprinted from *Shaw – 'The Chucker-Out'* (London, 1969), an assembly of his writings on a wide range of subjects. Editor Allan Chappelow cites the lecture as 'representative of numerous speeches on Socialism which Shaw made – always without fee, and often without even travelling expenses [...] during the five decades from the 1880s to the 1920s'.

In 1928, Shaw published a book entitled *The Intelligent Woman's Guide to Socialism and Capitalism*. It had taken him five years to write (during which he wrote no plays) and Shaw claimed it cost him his health, but he was pleased with the outcome and it sold well. The third series of extracts is from this book: on the changing role of women in 1920s English society; on his own personal experience of poverty and riches; and the clearest statement he ever made on eugenics, a topic on which he has been consistently misunderstood. The passage clearly shows that Shaw thought this noxious psuedo-science a nonsense.

The other means by which Shaw disseminated his socialism was through his plays. He followed on from fellow Irishman and socialist playwright Oscar Wilde in subjecting the English class system to critique, never more so than when Henry Higgins in *Pygmalion* (1914) shows that the accent on which the English base so many class differences is something that can readily be taught. Each of Shaw's plays works to expose the cash nexus on which power relations are based in the society being represented. Shaw's weapons for exposing that underlying reality are always comic.

Socialism holds that human nature can be altered amd improved. Socialist dramatists, consequently, are always comedians (Shaw and Wilde, but also Bertolt Brecht).

The tragedian believes that human nature is fated, given; the comic writer believes that it can be altered for the better.

A MANIFESTO

(FABIAN TRACTS NO. 2,

LONDON: 1884)

The Fabians are associated for the purpose of spreading the following opinions held by them, and discussing their practical consequences:

That, under existing circumstances, wealth cannot be enjoyed without dishonour, or foregone without misery.

That it is the duty of each member of the State to provide for his or her wants by his or her own Labour.

That a life-interest in the Land and Capital of the nation is the birth-right of every individual born within its confines; and that access to this birth-right should not depend upon the will of any private person other than the person seeking it.

That the most striking result of our present system of farming out the national Land and Capital to private individuals has been the division of Society into hostile classes, with large appetites and no dinners at one extreme, and large dinners and no appetites at the other.

That the practice of entrusting the Land of the nation to private persons in the hope that they will make the best of it has been discredited by the consistency with which they have made the worst of it; and that the Nationalisation of the Land in some form is a public duty.

That the pretensions of Capitalism to encourage Invention, and to distribute its benefits in the fairest way attainable, have been discredited by the experience of the nineteenth century.

That, under the existing system of leaving the National Industry to organize itself, Competition has the effect of rendering adulteration, dishonest dealing, and inhumanity compulsory.

That since Competition among producers admittedly secures to the public the most satisfactory products, the State should compete with all its might in every department of production.

That such restraints upon Free Competition as the penalties for infringing the Postal monopoly, and the withdrawal of workhouse and prison labour from the markets, should be abolished.

That no branch of Industry should be carried on at a profit by the central administration.

That the Public Revenue should be raised by a Direct Tax; and that the central administration should have no legal power to hold back for the replenishment of the Public Treasury any portion of the proceeds of the Industries administered by them.

That the State should compete with private individuals – especially with parents – in providing happy homes for children, so that every child may have a refuge from the tyranny or neglect of its natural custodians.

That Men no longer need special political privileges to protect them against Women; and that the sexes should henceforth enjoy equal political rights.

That no individual should enjoy any Privilege in consideration of services rendered to the State by his or her parents or other relations.

That the State should secure a liberal education and an equal share in the National Industry to each of its units.

That the established Government has no more right to call itself the State than the smoke of London has to call itself the weather.

That we had rather face a Civil War than such another century of suffering as the present one [the nineteenth century] has been.

LECTURE ON SOCIALISM

(1911)

It is becoming harder and harder for a man of my age [Shaw was fifty-five in that year] to get employment of any sort, even though he is still as able to work as I am able to talk at this present moment. But the more you get your industries into your own hands, and your land into your own hands, the more you will be in the employment of public, responsible bodies, controlled by your own votes. Public employment is the very best possible employment. You will notice that the middle classes spend a great deal of money in trying to get their sons into the Civil Service. They denounce Socialism for you, but are glad to avail themselves of it. They know the man in public employment has an absolutely safe berth, with a pension at the end of his service. He has no anxiety, and he is able to marry when twenty-three or twenty-four years of age, whereas the man in the Potteries cannot marry till forty, and very often not then.

There is also the question [...] of unemployment. I dare say all of you at this meeting have got a job, or you could not have paid to come into this room. Nevertheless, there is not a single one of you who may not be unemployed sooner than you think. The thing you have got to understand is this: That the man who is waiting for a job, and is willing to do it, has as good a right to be maintained and kept in good health and training as the man who is doing the job. (Cheers.) Look at your Army and your Navy. Supposing here, in England, we said: 'We will run our Navy in the same way that we run our ordinary affairs. We don't want to keep paying soldiers and feeding soldiers, and clothing soldiers, who have nothing to do but to eat their heads off. Throw them out into the streets.' Then when the Germans land next Tuesday, as the *Daily Mail* says, or some other paper which has taken up the cry – (laughter) – we can pay men from the streets sixpence an hour to go out armed to meet them. When the battle is over they can go back to the streets again. What chance would a country have that entrusted its national defence to such a silly system as that? You recognise, so far as your soldiers and police constables are concerned, that you have to keep them in good health and training, ready for the job which you only hope will never come. (Cheers and laughter.)

Will you ever realise that what you do with the military army you ought to do with the industrial army? (Renewed cheers.) When will you ratepayers realise that it does not pay you, to do what you do now? When you throw a man on the streets looking for a job, and leave him there for months, you have struck a mortal blow at that man's character. (Cheers.) It is from your unemployables that you get your criminals and your feeble-minded, and, as a result of your refraining from timely expenditure, you have in the long run to pay for police, for hospitals, and for all those things which ought not to exist in a properly conducted community. (Hear, hear.) It is not good commercial sense to do as you are now doing. (Cheers.)

[...]

If there is another life to come, if any man conceives that when this life is at an end that he will then go into the presence of God, who will ask him to give an account of his life, then he would not approach that God crawling, and asking for forgiveness of sins, and admitting he had lived in a wicked and horrible way. He would hold up his head even before his God and say: 'When I was in your world I did your work in the world. I did more than your work in the world; I left the world in my debt. You are in my debt. Now give me my reward!' (Concludes. Loud cheers.)

FROM *THE INTELLIGENT WOMAN'S GUIDE TO SOCIALISM AND CAPITALISM*

(1928)

WHAT WE SHOULD BUY FIRST

Beginning with industry, we are at once plunged into what we call political economy, to distinguish it from the domestic economy with which we are all only too familiar. Men find political economy a dry and difficult subject: they shirk it as they shirk housekeeping; yet it means nothing more abstruse than the art of managing a country as a housekeeper manages a house. If the men shirk it the women must tackle it. The nation has a certain income to manage on just as a housekeeper has: and the problem is how to spend that income to the greatest general advantage. [...] The only way in which a nation can make itself wealthy and prosperous is by good housekeeping: that is, by providing for its wants in the order of their importance, and allowing no money to be wasted on whims and luxuries until necessities have been thoroughly served.

THE MIDDLE STATION IN LIFE

Nowadays, there are far more careers open to women. We have women barristers and women doctors in practice. True, the Church is closed against them, to its own great detriment, as it could easily find picked women, eloquent in the pulpit and capable in parish management, to replace the male refuse it has too often to fall back on; but women can do without ecclesiastical careers now that the secular and civil service are open. The closing of the fighting services [to women] is socially necessary as women are far too valuable to have their lives risked in battle as well as in childbearing. If ninety out of every hundred young men were killed, we could recover from the loss, but if ninety out of every hundred young women were killed there would be an end of the nation. That is why modern war, which is not confined to battlefields, and rains high explosives and poison gas on male and female civilians indiscriminately in their peaceful homes, is so much more dangerous than war has ever been before. Besides, women are now educated as men are: they go to the universities and to the technical colleges if they can afford it; and, as Domestic Service is now an educational subject with special colleges, a woman can get trained for such an occupation as that of manageress of a hotel as well as for the practice of law or medicine, or for accountancy or actuarial work. In short, nothing now blocks a woman's way into business or professional life except prejudice, superstition, old-fashioned parents, shyness, snobbery, ignorance of the contemporary world and all the other imbecilities for which there is no remedy but modern ideas and force of character.

CAPITALISM

You had better know whom you are dealing with. I am a landlord and capitalist, rich enough to be supertaxed; and in addition I have a special sort of property called literary property, for the use of which I charge people exactly as a landlord charges rent for his land. I object to inequality of income not as a man with a small income, but as one with a middling big one. But I know what it is to be a proletarian, and a poor one at that. I have worked in an office and I have pulled through years of professional unemployment, some of the hardest of them at the expense of my mother. I have known the extremes of failure and of success. The class in which I was born was that most unlucky of all classes: the class that claims gentility and is expected to keep up its appearances without more than the barest scrap and remnant of property to do it on. I intrude these confidences on you because it is as well that you be able to allow for my personal bias. The rich often write about the poor, and the poor about the rich, without really knowing what they are writing about. I know the whole gamut from personal experience, short of actual hunger and homelessness, which should never be experienced by anybody. If I cry sour grapes, you need not suspect that they are only out of my reach: they are all in my hand at their ripest and best.

EUGENICS

There are some who say that if you want better people you must breed them as carefully as you breed thorough-bred horses and pedigree boars. No doubt you must; but there are two difficulties. First, you cannot very well mate men and women as you mate bulls and cows, stallions and mares, boars and sows, without giving them any choice in the matter. Second, even if you could, you would not know [...] what sort of human being you wanted to breed. In the case of a horse or a pig the matter is very simple: you want either a very fast horse for racing or a very strong horse for drawing loads; and in the case of the pig you want simply plenty of bacon.

And yet, simple as that is, any breeder of these animals will tell you that he has a great many failures no matter how careful he is.

The moment you ask yourself what sort of child you want, beyond preferring a boy or a girl, you have to confess that you do not know. At best you can mention a few sorts that you don't want: for instance you don't want cripples, deaf mutes, blind, imbecile, epileptic or drunken children. But even these you do not know how to avoid, as there is often nothing visibly wrong with the parents of such unfortunates. When you turn from what you don't want to what you do want you may say that you want good children; but a good child means only a child that gives its parents no trouble; and some very useful men and women have been very troublesome children. Energetic, imaginative, enterprising, brave children are never out of mischief from their parents' point of view. And grown-up geniuses are seldom liked until they are dead. Considering that we poisoned Socrates, crucified Christ and burnt Joan of Arc amid popular applause, because, after a trial by responsible lawyers and Churchmen, we decided that they were too wicked to be allowed to live, we can hardly set up to be judges of goodness or to have any sincere liking for it.

Even if we were willing to trust any political authority to select our husbands and wives for us with a view
to improving the race, the officials would be hopelessly
puzzled as to how to select. They might begin with some
rough idea of preventing the marriage of persons with
any taint of consumption or madness or syphilis or addic-
tion to drugs or drink in their families; but that would
end in nobody being married at all, as there is practi-
cally no family quite free from such taints. As to moral
excellence, what model would they take as desirable? St.
Francis, George Fox, William Penn, John Wesley and
George Washington? Or Alexander, Caesar, Napoleon
and Bismarck? It takes all sorts to make a world, and the
notion of a Government department trying to make out
how many different types were necessary, and how many
persons of each type, and proceeding to breed them by
appropriate marriages, is amusing but not practicable.
There is nothing for it but to let people choose their
mates for themselves, and trust to Nature to produce a
good result.

Shaw in his mid-thirties:
Portrait of the Artist as a
Young Professional.

CHAPTER TWO

IDEALISM
AND
REALISM

THE PROSE AND PLAYS OF THE 1890S

THE QUINTESSENCE OF IBSENISM

(1891, 1913, 1922)

The staging of Henrik Ibsen's play *A Doll's House* in London in 1889 caused a scandal, only exceeded by the uproar which greeted his *Ghosts* a few years later. The two London theatre critics who supported the infamous Norwegian playwright were Ibsen's English translator, William Archer, and the Irishman Bernard Shaw. In 1891, Shaw wrote an essay, 'The Quintessence of Ibsenism', which sought to defend and define Ibsen's radical originality as thinker and playwright.

Shaw characteristically opened with an ironic move, by agreeing with the most extreme of Ibsen's critics, and going on to argue that Ibsen was deadly serious in attacking the most cherished of social institutions, like the family and marriage, in *A Doll's House*. He did so to tear away the mask of idealism, the self-deceiving lies with which people sought to blind themselves to reality.

That urge to revolution Shaw saw as ultimately religious in inspiration; and he brilliantly concludes the long essay on Ibsen by declaring the man most people regarded as a blasphemer to be a religious reformer.

The technical feature that Shaw saw as central to the plays of Ibsen was the emphasis on the discussion. For him, *A Doll's House* moves into new dramatic territory when Nora Helmer turns to her husband in the final act and says: 'We must sit down and discuss all that has been happening between us.' Shaw points out that plays have been written since in which 'the discussion interpenetrates the action from beginning to end'; in so doing he provides a succinct paradigm of what was to be his own dramatic practice.

FROM THE QUINTESSENCE OF IBSENISM

The statement that Ibsen's plays have an immoral tendency is, in the sense in which it is used, quite true. Immorality does not necessarily imply mischievous conduct: it implies conduct, mischievous or not, which does not conform to current ideals. All religions begin with a revolt against morality, and perish when morality conquers them and stamps out such words as grace and sin, substituting for them morality and immorality. [John] Bunyan [in *The Pilgrim's Progress*] places the town of Morality, with its respectable leading citizens Mr. Legality and Mr. Civility, close to the City of Destruction. In the United States today he would be imprisoned for this. Born as I was in the seventeenth century atmosphere of mid-nineteenth century Ireland, I can remember when men who talked about morality were suspected of reading Tom Paine, if not of being downright atheists. Ibsen's attack on morality is a symptom of the revival of religion, not of its extinction. He is on the side of the prophets in having devoted himself to showing that the spirit or will of Man is constantly outgrowing the ideals, and that therefore thoughtless conformity to them is constantly producing results no less tragic than those which follow thoughtless violation of them.

[...]

To this day [critics] remain blind to a new technical factor in the art of popular stage-play making which every considerable playwright has been thrusting under their noses night after night for a whole generation. This technical factor in the play is the discussion.

Formerly you had in what was called a well made play an exposition in the first act, a situation in the second, and unravelling in the third. Now you have exposition, situation, and discussion; and the discussion is the test of the playwright. The critics protest in vain. They declare that discussions are not dramatic, and that art should not be didactic. Neither the playwrights nor the public take the smallest notice of them. The discussion conquered Europe in Ibsen's *Doll's House*; and now the serious playwright recognizes in the discussion not only the main test of his highest powers, but also the real centre of his play's interest.

[...]

Hence a cry has arisen that the post-Ibsen play is not a play, and that its technique, not being the technique described by Aristotle, is not a technique at all. I will not enlarge on this: the fun poked at my friend Mr. A.B. Walkley in the proloogue of *Fanny's First Play* need not be repeated here. But I may remind him that the new technique is new only on the modern stage. It has been used by preachers and orators ever since speech was invented. It is the technique of playing upon the human conscience; and it has been practised by the playwright whenever the playwright has been capable of it. Rhetoric, irony, argument, paradox, epigram, parable, the rearrangement of haphazard facts into orderly and intelligent situations: these are both the oldest and the newest arts of the drama.

ARMS AND THE MAN

(1894)

Shaw carried the conflict of idealism and realism that he derived from Ibsen forward into the plays he wrote in the 1890s. In 1898 these were gathered together and published collectively under the titles *Plays Pleasant* and *Plays Unpleasant*. In the 'unpleasant' plays, the mask of idealism the characters hid behind was ripped off to confront the harsh economic facts underneath: slum landlordism in *Widowers' Houses* (1892) and prostitution in *Mrs Warren's Profession* (1893). The 'pleasant' plays, such as *Arms and the Man* (1894) and *You Never Can Tell* (1896), still presented the conflict between idealism and realism, but in a more good-humoured vein, one that played with but did not finally subvert the dramatic conventions of romantic comedy. In *Arms and the Man*, the courtship between Raina and Sergius is played out in the high romantic vein. The intrusion of Captain Bluntschli into Raina's life brings a bracing dose of reality, which she benefits from and even comes to appreciate. The philandering Sergius is brought to heel by the sexy, tough-minded maid Louka and agrees to marry her. The 'unpleasant' plays, not surprisingly, failed to find favour with the Lord Chamberlain's readers and were denied production: they were deliberate weapons in Shaw's lifelong battle against stage censorship. The 'pleasant' plays were immediately and successfully staged in London.

Arms and the Man was Shaw's first great success in the theatre. Put on by the actress Florence Farr and funded by Annie Horniman, who would later pay for Dublin's Abbey Theatre, *Arms and the Man* played at the Avenue Theatre, London, on 21 April 1894 with WB Yeats's *The Land of Heart's Desire* as a curtain-raiser. When the audience's cheers summoned Shaw to the stage, a lone heckler at the back began to boo loudly. Shaw's riposte was immediate: 'I assure the gentleman in the gallery that he and I are of exactly the same opinion, but what can we do against a whole house who are of the contrary opinion?' Yeats, who was watching from the wings, confirms that this night established Shaw's reputation both as a playwright and a public speaker: 'From that moment Bernard Shaw became the most formidable man in modern letters, and even the most drunken of medical students knew it.'

FROM
ARMS AND THE MAN

FROM ACT TWO

RAINA. I will get my hat; and then we can go out until lunch time. Wouldn't you like that?

SERGIUS. Be quick. If you are away five minutes, it will seem five hours. [*Raina runs to the top of the steps, and turns there to exchange looks with him and wave him a kiss with both hands. He looks after her with emotion for a moment; then turns slowly away, his face radiant with the loftiest exaltation. The movement shifts his field of vision, into the corner of which there now comes the tail of Louka's double apron. His attention is arrested at once. He takes a stealthy look at her, and begins to twirl his moustache mischievously, with his left hand akimbo on his hip. Finally, striking the ground with his heels in something of a cavalry swagger, he strolls over to the other side of the table, opposite her, and says*]

Louka: do you know what the higher love is? –

LOUKA [*astonished*] No, sir.

SERGIUS. Very fatiguing thing to keep up for any length of

time, Louka. One feels the need for some relief after it.

LOUKA [*innocently*] Perhaps you would like some coffee,
sir? [*She stretches her hand across the table for the coffee pot*].

SERGIUS [*taking her hand*] Thank you, Louka.

LOUKA [*pretending to pull*] Oh, sir, you know I didn't
mean that. I'm surprised at you!

SERGIUS [*coming clear of the table and drawing her with
him*] I am surprised at myself, Louka. What would
Sergius, the hero of Slivnitza, say if he saw me now?
What would Sergius, the apostle of the higher love,
say if he saw me now? What would the half dozen
Sergiuses who keep popping in and out of this handsome figure of mine say if they caught us here? [*Letting
go her hand and slipping his arm dexterously round her
waist*] Do you consider my figure handsome, Louka?

LOUKA. Let me go, sir. I shall be disgraced. [*She struggles:
he holds her inexorably*] Oh, will you let go?

SERGIUS [*looking straight into her eyes*] No.

LOUKA. Then stand back where we can't be seen. Have
you no common sense?

FROM ACT THREE

RAINA. [My father and Sergius] don't know that it was in
this house you took refuge. If Sergius knew, he would
challenge you and kill you in a duel.

BLUNTSCHLI. Bless me! then don't tell him.

RAINA. Please be serious, Captain Bluntschli. Can you
not realise what it is to me to deceive him? I want to
be quite perfect with Sergius: no meanness, no small-
ness, no deceit. My relation to him is the one really
beautiful and noble part of my life. I hope you can
understand that.

BLUNTSCHLI [*sceptically*] You mean that you wouldn't
like him to find out that the story about the ice pudding
was a – a – a – You know.

RAINA [*wincing*] Ah, don't talk of it in that flippant
way. I lied: I know it. But I did it to save your life.
He would have killed you. That was the second time
I ever uttered a falsehood. [*Bluntschli rises quickly and
looks doubtfully and somewhat severely at her*] Do you
remember the first time?

BLUNTSCHLI. I! No. Was I present?

RAINA. Yes; and I told the officer who was searching for
you that you were not present.

BLUNTSCHLI. True. I should have remembered it. [...]
You said you'd told only two lies in your whole life.
Dear young lady: isn't that rather a short allowance? I'm
quite a straightforward man myself; but it wouldn't last
me a whole morning.

RAINA [*staring haughtily at him*] Do you know, sir, that you are insulting me?

BLUNTSCHLI. I can't help it. When you strike that noble attitude and speak in that thrilling voice, I admire you; but I find it impossible to believe a single word you say.

RAINA [*superbly*] Captain Bluntschli!

BLUNTSCHLI [*unmoved*] Yes?

RAINA [*standing over him, as if she could not believe her senses*] Do you mean what you said just now? Do you know what you said just now?

BLUNTSCHLI. I do.

RAINA [gasping] I! I!!! [*She points to herself incredulously, meaning 'I, Raina Petkoff tell lies!' He meets her gaze unflinchingly. She suddenly sits down beside him, and adds, with a complete change of manner from the heroic to a babyish familiarity*] How did you find me out?

BLUNTSCHLI [*promptly*] Instinct, dear young lady. Instinct, and experience of the world.

RAINA [*wonderingly*] Do you know, you are the first man I ever met who did not take me seriously?

BLUNTSCHLI. You mean, don't you, that I am the first man that has ever taken you quite seriously?

MRS WARREN'S PROFESSION

(1893, 1902)

Shaw's socialism naturally found common cause with the burgeoning feminism of the 1890s, with the rise of the suffragette movement and the emergence of the New Woman to challenge gender stereotypes. The young Vivie Warren is a New Woman. She has been well educated (with a recent First in Mathematics from Cambridge), smokes, dresses rationally and has an eye on pursuing a career in law.

As Shaw wrote about the play: 'I simply affirm that *Mrs Warren's Profession* is a play for women; that it was written for women; that it has been performed and produced mainly through the determination of women; that the enthusiasm of women made its first performance excitingly successful; and that not one of these women had any inducement to support it except their belief in the timeliness and power of the lesson the play teaches.'

Shaw repeatedly made the point that his objection was not to a prostitute like Mrs Warren, who runs a string of brothels on the Continent unbeknownst to her daughter.

Rather, the focus of his attack was the capitalist system that created prostitution by underpaying and overworking women so shockingly in almost all other areas of female employment.

The idea for Vivie came from Beatrice Webb, a lifelong friend and collaborator in the Fabian Society, 'one whose knowledge of English social types is as remarkable as her command of industrial and political questions'. Beatrice Webb 'suggested that I should put on the stage a real modern lady of the governing class'.

The mother and daughter are central to the play; the men mere satellites who float about to no great purpose (the young male romantic lead is 'charming but worthless'). At its dramatic heart are two lengthy, emotionally charged scenes between Mrs Warren and Vivie.

FROM MRS WARREN'S PROFESSION

FROM ACT TWO

MRS WARREN. Oh, it's easy to talk, very easy, isn't it? Here! Would you like to know what my circumstances were?

VIVIE.Yes, you had better tell me. Won't you sit down?

MRS WARREN. Oh, I'll sit down: don't you be afraid.

[*She plants her chair further forward with brazen energy, and sits down. Vivie is impressed in spite of herself*]. D'you know what your gran'mother was?

VIVIE. No.

MRS WARREN. No you don't. I do. She called herself a widow and had a fried-fish shop down by the Mint, and kept herself and four daughters out of it. Two of us were sisters: that was me and Liz; and we were both good-looking and well made. I suppose our father was a well-fed man; mother pretended he was a gentleman; but I don't know. The other two were only half sisters: undersized, ugly, starved looking, hard working, honest poor creatures: Liz and I would have half-murdered them if mother hadn't half-murdered us to keep our hands off them. They were the respectable ones. Well, what did they get by their respectability? I'll tell you. One of them worked in a whitelead factory twelve hours a day for nine shillings a week until she died of lead poisoning. She only expected to get her hands a little paralyzed; but she died. The other was always held up to us as a model because she married a Government labourer in the Deptford victualling yard, and kept his room and the three children neat and tidy on eighteen shillings a week – until he took to drink. That was worth being respectable for, wasn't it?

VIVIE [*now thoughtfully attentive*] Did you and your sister think so?

MRS WARREN. Liz didn't, I can tell you; she had more spirit. We both went to a church school – that was part of the ladylike airs we gave ourselves to be superior to the children that knew nothing and went nowhere – and we stayed there until Liz went out one night and never came back. [...] Then I was a waitress; and then I went to the bar at Waterloo Station: fourteen hours a day serving drinks and washing glasses for four shillings a week and my board. That was considered a great promotion for me. Well, one cold, wretched night, when I was so tired I could hardly keep myself awake, who should come up for a half of Scotch but Lizzie, in a long fur cloak, elegant and comfortable, with a lot of sovereigns in her purse.

VIVIE [*grimly*] My aunt Lizzie!

MRS WARREN. Yes; and a very good aunt to have, too. She's living down at Winchester now, close to the cathedral, one of the most respectable ladies there. Chaperones girls at the county ball, if you please. No river for Liz, thank you!

You remind me of Liz a little: she was a first-rate business woman – saved money from the beginning – never let herself look too like what she was – never lost her head or threw away a chance. When she saw I'd grown up good-looking she said to me across the bar 'What are you doing there, you little fool? Wearing out your health and your appearance for other people's profit!' Liz was saving money then to take a house for herself in Brussels; and she thought we two could save faster than one. So she lent me some money and gave me a start; and I saved steadily and first paid her back; and then went into business with her as my partner. Why shouldn't I have done it? The house in Brussels was real high class: a much better place for a woman to be in than the factory where Aunt Jane got poisoned. None of our girls were ever treated as I was treated in the scullery of that temperance place, or at the Waterloo bar, or at home. Would you have had me stay in them and become a worn out old drudge before I was forty?

FROM ACT FOUR

VIVIE. Tell me why you continue your business now that you are independent of it. Your sister, you told me, has left all that behind her. Why don't you do the same?

MRS WARREN. Oh, it's all very easy for Liz: she
likes good society, and has the air of being a lady.
Imagine me in a cathedral town! Why, the very
rooks in the trees would find me out even if I could
stand the dullness of it. I must have work and
excitement, or I should go melancholy mad. And
what else is there for me to do? The life suits me:
I'm fit for it and not for anything else. If I didn't
do it somebody else would; so I don't do any real
harm by it. And then it brings in money; and I like
making money. No: it's no use: I can't give it up –
not for anybody. But what need you know about it?
I'll never mention it. I'll keep Crofts away. I'll not
trouble you much; you see I have to be constantly
running about from one place to another. You'll be
quit of me altogether when I die.

VIVIE. No: I am my mother's daughter. I am like you: I
must have work, and must make more money than I
spend. But my work is not your work, and my way not
your way. We must part. [...]

MRS WARREN. I was a good mother; and because I
made my daughter a good woman she turns me out as
if I was a leper. [...]

VIVIE. If I had been you, mother, I might have done
as you did; but I should not have lived one life and

believed in another. You are a conventional woman at heart. That is why I am bidding you goodbye now. I am right, am I not?

MRS WARREN [*taken aback*] Right to throw away all my money?

VIVIE. No: right to get rid of you? I should be a fool not to! Isn't that so?

MRS WARREN [*sulkily*] Oh well, yes, if you come to that, I suppose you are. But Lord help the world if everybody took to doing the right thing!

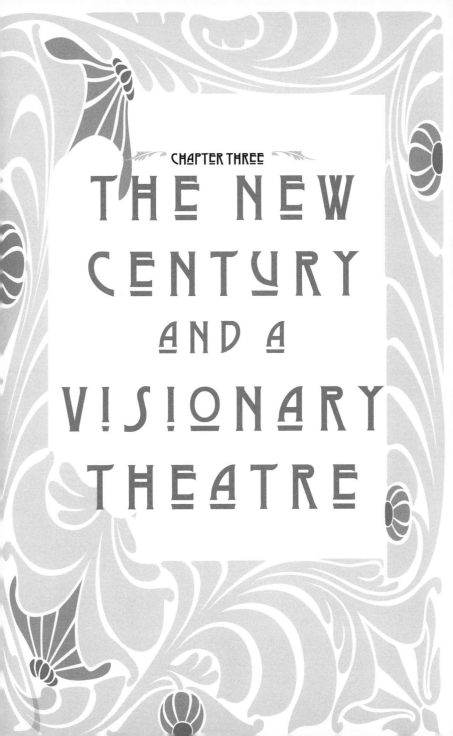

CHAPTER THREE

THE NEW CENTURY AND A VISIONARY THEATRE

Shaw and Charlotte Payne-Townshend, his Irish wife and life-partner in all his enterprises.

MEN AND WOMEN

MAN AND SUPERMAN

(1901-03)

In an epistle to his good friend and fellow theatre critic Arthur Walkley, Shaw describes *Man and Superman* as a Don Juan play. And yet far from pursuing young women, Jack Tanner appears to have little interest in them and, where the beautiful Ann Whitefield is concerned, to run as energetically as possible in the opposite direction. What Tanner most embodies from Don Juan's character is his revolutionary spirit, his iconoclasm in speaking out against conventional creeds.

The pursuit of the opposite sex associated with Don Juan is centrally present in the play, but, in a characteristically Shavian inversion, the woman is now the pursuer, the man the pursued. Since being a sexual predator does not comport with being a well-reared young woman, Ann Whitefield has to disguise her agency behind a facade of always doing her duty, whether to her recently dead father or to her increasingly exasperated mother, who knows only too well what her daughter is up to.

Jack protests loudly to the very end of the play that he does not want to marry Ann – or anyone – because to do so would be to compromise and lose his independence of spirit. But the fascination proves too great and Jack finally has to succumb and declare unequivocally to Ann that 'I love you' – the most delayed and hard-won such declaration in the history of romantic comedy.

The play was Shaw's first great success at the Royal Court Theatre, with Harley Granville-Barker as Jack Tanner, and was followed there by *John Bull's Other Island* and *Major Barbara*. With these three great visionary plays, Shaw's new and more ambitious kind of theatre launched forth confidently into the twentieth century.

FROM
MAN AND SUPERMAN

FROM ACT ONE

ANN. Why did you break off our confidences and become quite strange to me?

TANNER [*enigmatically*] It happened just then that I got something that I wanted to keep all to myself instead of sharing it with you.

ANN. I am sure I shouldn't have asked for any of it if you had grudged it.

TANNER. It wasn't a box of sweets, Ann. It was something you'd never have let me call my own.

ANN [*incredulously*] What?

TANNER. My soul.

ANN. Oh, do be sensible, Jack. You know you're talking nonsense.

TANNER. The most solemn earnest, Ann. You didn't notice at that time that you were getting a soul too. But you were. [...]

ANN. Why do you persist in thinking me so narrow minded?

TANNER. That's the danger of it. I know you don't mind, because you've found out that it doesn't matter. The boa constrictor doesn't mind the opinions of a stag one little bit when once she has got her coils round it.

ANN [*rising in sudden enlightenment*] O – o – o – o – oh! Now I understand why you warned Tavy that I am a boa constrictor. Granny told me. [*She laughs and throws her boa round his neck*] Doesn't it feel nice and soft, Jack?

TANNER [*in the toils*] You scandalous woman, will you throw away even your hypocrisy?

ANN. I am never hypocritical with you, Jack. Are you angry? [*She withdraws the boa and throws it on a chair*]. Perhaps I shouldn't have done that.

TANNER [*contemptuously*] Pooh, prudery! Why should you not, if it amuses you?

ANN [*shyly*] Well, because – because I suppose what you really meant by the boa constrictor was this [*she puts her arms round his neck*].

TANNER [*staring at her*] Magnificent audacity! [*She laughs and pats his cheeks*]

FROM ACT FOUR

[*Set in Granada*]

ANN. You ought to get married.

TANNER [*explosively*] Ann: I will not marry you. Do you hear, I won't, won't, won't, won't, WON'T marry you.

ANN [*placidly*] Well, nobody axd you, sir she said, sir she said, sir she said. So that's settled.

TANNER. Yes, nobody has asked me; but everybody treats the thing as settled. It's in the air. When we meet, the others go away on absurd pretexts to leave us alone together. Ramsden [Ann's guardian] no longer scowls at me: his eye beams, as if he were already giving you away to me in church. Tavy [Ann's other suitor] refers me to your mother and gives me his blessing. Straker [Tanner's chauffeur] openly treats you as his future employer: it was he who first told me of it.

ANN. Was that why you ran away?

TANNER. Yes... [...]

ANN. Well, if you don't want to be married, you needn't be [*she turns away from him and sits down, much at her ease*].

TANNER [*following her*] Does any man want to be hanged? Yet men let themselves be hanged without a struggle for life, though they could at least give the chaplain a black eye. We do the world's will, not our own. I have a frightful feeling that I shall let myself be married because it is the world's will that you should have a husband.

ANN. I dare say I shall, someday.

TANNER. But why me? Me of all men! Marriage is to me apostasy, profanation of the sanctuary of my soul, violation of my manhood, sale of my birthright, shameful surrender, ignominious capitulation, acceptance of defeat. [...]

I will not marry you. I will not marry you.

ANN. Oh, you will, you will.

TANNER. I tell you, no, no, no.

ANN. I tell you, yes, yes, yes.

TANNER. No.

ANN [*coaxing – imploring – almost exhausted*] Yes. Before it is too late for repentance. Yes.

TANNER [*struck by an echo from the past*] When did all this happen to me before? Are we two dreaming?

ANN [*Suddenly losing her courage, with an anguish that she does not conceal*] No. We are awake; and you have said no: that is all.

TANNER [*brutally*] Well?

ANN. Well, I made a mistake: you do not love me.

TANNER [*seizing her in his arms*] It is false. I love you. The Life Force enchants me: I have the whole world in my arms when I clasp you. But I am fighting for my life, for my honour, for my self, one and indivisible.

ANN. Your happiness will be worth them all.

TANNRR. You would sell freedom and honour and self for happiness?

ANN. It will not be all happiness. Perhaps death.

TANNER [*groaning*] Oh, that clutch holds and hurts. What have you grasped in me? Is there a father's heart as well as a mother's?

ANN. Take care, Jack: if anyone comes while we are like this, you will have to marry me.

TANNER. If we two stood now on the edge of a precipice, I would hold you tight and jump.

IRELAND AND ENGLAND

JOHN BULL'S OTHER ISLAND (1904)

When WB Yeats and Lady Gregory commissioned a new play from Shaw for the opening of the Abbey Theatre in Dublin on 26 December 1904, he sat down and wrote about the native country he had left some twenty-eight years earlier, probing the complex relations between Ireland and England with wit, passion and political intelligence.

Yeats was quick to recognise how deeply Shaw had delved: 'You have said things in this play which are entirely true about Ireland, things which nobody has ever said before, and these are the very things that are most part of the action. It astonishes me that you should have been so long in London and yet have remembered so much. To some extent this play is unlike anything you have done before. Hitherto you have taken your situations from melodrama, and called up logic to make them ridiculous. Your process here seems to be quite different, you are taking your situations more from life, you are for the first time trying to get the atmosphere of a place, you have for the first time a geographical conscience.'

However, the objections to *John Bull* accumulated on the Abbey side: it was 'immensely too long' and Shaw's efforts to cut it proved unavailing. The Abbey's limited theatrical resources were not up to the complex demands of staging the play; a suitable cast would be hard to find. In the end, the play was rejected by the new National Theatre.

Shaw did not hang about. Harley Granville-Barker was ready to stage it in London at the Royal Court on 1 November 1904, with a practised ensemble. As Shaw notes in his Preface, 'the production of the play in London at the Court Theatre by Messrs [J.E.] Vedrenne and Barker' met with 'an immediate and enormous popularity which delighted and flattered English audiences.' Among the attendees was King Edward, who came to see it twice.

Three years later, back in Dublin, a touring production of *John Bull* by the Barker-Vedrenne Company played to a packed Theatre Royal while the Abbey's latest offerings from Yeats and Gregory drew small houses. The irony was not lost on the Abbey Theatre's directors. *John Bull's Other Island* was finally produced at the Abbey at Lady Gregory's prompting in 1916, and had an annual production every year thereafter until 1936.

FROM 'PREFACE FOR POLITICIANS' (1906)

John Bull's Other Island was written in 1904 at the request of Mr William Butler Yeats, as a patriotic contribution to the repertory of the Irish Literary Theatre. Like most people who have asked me to write plays, Mr Yeats got rather more than he bargained for. The play was at that time beyond the resources of the new Abbey Theatre, which the Irish enterprise owed to the public spirit of Miss A.E.F. Horniman (an Englishwoman, of course), who, twelve years ago, played an important part in the history of the English stage as well as in my own personal destiny by providing the necessary capital for that memorable season at the Avenue Theatre which forced my *Arms and the Man* and Mr. Yeats's *Land of Heart's Desire* on the recalcitrant London playgoer. [...]

There was another reason for changing the destination of *John Bull's Other Island* [from Dublin to London]. It was uncongenial to the whole spirit of the neo-Gaelic movement, which is bent on creating a new Ireland after its own ideal, whereas my play is a very uncompromising presentment of the real old Ireland.

FROM *JOHN BULL'S OTHER ISLAND*

LARRY DOYLE [*With sudden anguish*] Rosscullen! Oh, good Lord, Rosscullen! The dullness! The hopelessness! The ignorance! The bigotry!

TOM BROADBENT [*matter-of-factly*] The usual thing in the country, Larry. Just the same here.

DOYLE [*hastily*] No, no: the climate is different. Here [in London], if the life is dull, you can be dull too, and no great harm done. [*Going off into a passionate dream*] But your wits can't thicken in that soft moist air, on those white springy roads, in those misty rushes and brown bogs, on those hillsides of granite rocks and magenta heather. You've no such colours in the sky, no such lure in the distances, no such sadness in the evenings. Oh, the dreaming! The dreaming! The torturing, heart-scalding, never satisfying dreaming, dreaming, dreaming, dreaming! [*Savagely*] No debauchery that ever coarsened and brutalised an Englishman can take the worth and usefulness out of him like that dreaming. An Irishman's imagination never lets him alone, never convinces him, never satisfies him; but it makes him that he can't face reality nor deal with it nor handle it nor conquer it: he can only sneer at them that do, and [*bitterly, at Broadbent*] be 'agreeable to strangers', like a good-for-nothing woman on the streets. [*Gabbling at Broadbent across the table*] It's all dreaming, all imagination. He cannot be religious. The inspired Churchman that teaches him the sanctity of life and the importance of conduct is sent away empty; while the poor village priest that gives him a miracle or a sentimental story of a saint, has cathedrals built for him out of the pennies of the poor. He can't be intelligently political: he dreams of what the Shan Van Vocht said in ninety-eight. If you want to interest him in Ireland you've got to call the unfortunate island Kathleen ní Houlihan and pretend she's a little old woman. It saves thinking. It saves working. It saves everything except imagination, imagination, imagination; and imagination's such a torture that you can't bear it without whisky. [...]

BROADBENT. You know, all this sounds rather interesting. There's the Irish charm about it. That's the worst of you: the Irish charm doesn't exist for you.

DOYLE. Oh yes it does. But it's the charm of a dream. Live in contact with dreams and you will get something of their charm: live in contact with facts and you will get something of their brutality. I wish I could find a country to live in where the facts were not brutal and the dreams not unreal.

POVERTY

MAJOR BARBARA (1905)

By 1905, Oscar Wilde was five years dead. But Shaw's play *Major Barbara* is a profound engagement with the legacy of Wilde, measuring itself against him and seeking not so much to rewrite as to go beyond him. The first act takes place between the four walls of one of the wealthy drawing-rooms in which all of Oscar Wilde's comedies are set. It is presided over by Lady Britomart, close kin to Wilde's Lady Bracknell, who delivers the same dismissive barbs at her daughter's simpering intended as Lady Bracknell does at her nephew Algernon: 'You don't think, Charles. You never do; and the result is, you never mean anything.'

The play begins as a Wildean romantic comedy, confronting the young lovers with obstacles that prevent them from marrying. But it expands from this conventional model when it comes to one of the young women, Barbara. A major in the Salvation Army, she challenges gender norms by adopting masculine dress and as a high-ranking military officer who wields authority.

When the play moves outdoors to the Salvation Army's West Ham shelter in Act Two, it presents a vision of squalor and poverty, with which Shaw was well acquainted in both Dublin and London. This was a scene of social reality from which he thought Wilde had averted his gaze. The play is also complicated by the appearance in Act One of the long-missing father, the arms manufacturer Andrew Undershaft. Act Three moves from the present to the future and into a visionary mode, disclosing the scene of Undershaft's munitions factory, not as a smoky, nineteenth-century furnace, but as a gleaming model of futuristic efficiency.

Here too, however, Wilde had pointed the way, not in his plays but in his prose work 'The Soul of Man Under Socialism' (1891). Wilde was inspired to write this essay after hearing Shaw speak at a Fabian meeting. Although Wilde may finally insist on a heightened individuality as the desired outcome of socialism, both Irish writers agree on a detestation of poverty as the ultimate degradation of the human spirit and recognise that no social progress is possible unless and until poverty is completely eliminated.

As Wilde puts it: 'The proper aim is to try and reconstruct society on such a basis that poverty will be impossible.'

If Act One of *Major Barbara* replicates one of Wilde's stage comedies, the blueprint for Acts Two and Three of Shaw's play are in the following lines from 'The Soul of Man Under Socialism': 'And when scientific men are no longer called upon to go down to a depressing East End and distribute bad cocoa and worse blankets to starving people there will be great storages of force for every city and this force man will convert into heat, light or motion, according to his needs. Is this Utopian? Progress is the realisation of Utopias.' It was a sentiment Shaw could endorse.

FROM
MAJOR BARBARA

CUSINS. Do you call poverty a crime?

UNDERSHAFT. The worst of crimes. All the other crimes are virtues beside it: all the other dishonours are chivalry itself by comparison. Poverty blights whole cities; spreads horrible pestilences; strikes dead the very souls of all who come within sight, sound or smell of it. What you call crime is nothing: a murder here and a theft there, a blow now and a curse then: what do they matter? They are only the accidents and illnesses of life: there are not fifty genuine professional criminals in London. But there are millions of poor people, abject people, dirty people, ill fed, ill clothed people. They poison us morally and physically; they kill the happiness of society: they force us to do away with our own liberties and to organise unnatural cruelties for fear they should rise against us and drag us down into their abyss. Only fools fear crime: we all fear poverty. Pah! [*turning on Barbara*] You talk of your half-saved ruffian in West Ham: you accuse me of dragging his soul back to perdition. Well, bring him to me here; and I will drag his soul back again to salvation for you. Not by words and dreams; but by thirty-eight shillings a week, a sound house in a handsome street, and a permanent job. In three weeks he will have a fancy waistcoat; in three months a tall hat and a chapel sitting; before the end of the year he will shake hands with a duchess at a Primrose League meeting, and join the Conservative Party.

BARBARA. And will he be the better for that?

UNDERSHAFT. You know he will. Don't be a hypocrite, Barbara. He will be better fed, better housed, better clothed, better behaved; and his children will be pounds heavier and bigger. That will be better than an American cloth mattress in a shelter, chopping firewood, eating bread and treacle, and being forced to kneel down from time to time to thank heaven for it: knee drill, I think you call it. It is cheap work converting starving men with a Bible in one hand and a slice of bread in the other. I will undertake to convert West Ham to Mahometanism on the same terms. Try your hand on my men: their souls are hungry because their bodies are full.

BARBARA. And leave the east end to starve?

UNDERSHAFT [*his energetic tone dropping into one of bitter and brooding remembrance*] *I* was an east ender. I moralised and starved until one day I swore that I would be a full-fed free man at all costs; that nothing should stop me except a bullet, neither reason nor morals nor the lives of other men. I said 'Thou shalt starve ere I starve'; and with that word I became free and great. I was a dangerous man until I had my will: now I am a useful, benificent, kindly person. That is the history of most self-made millionaires, I fancy. When it is the history of every Englishman we shall have an England worth living in.

LADY BRITOMART. Stop making speeches, Andrew. This is not the place for them.

UNDERSHAFT [*punctured*] My dear: I have no other means of conveying my ideas.

CHAPTER FOUR

FLOWER
GIRLS
AND
DUCHESSES

A radiant Mrs Patrick Campbell, the first and greatest performer of Eliza Doolittle, thirty-one years her junior.

PYGMALION (1914, 1938) AND MY FAIR LADY (1956, 1963)

*P*ygmalion opened at Sir Herbert Beerbohm Tree's His Majesty's Theatre in London on 11 April 1914. Tree both directed and played Henry Higgins; but the star turn was Mrs Patrick Campbell as Eliza Doolittle. Mrs Pat, as she was known, was then forty-nine years of age; Eliza is eighteen. But the beautiful and charismatic actress was a sensation in the part.

Mrs Pat's beauty captivated Shaw when he first read her the play, and they entered into a love affair which stopped just short of consummation – by the time Shaw presented himself at her hotel door in Sandwich, she had fled back to London. His letter to her on the occasion is a masterpiece of wounded amour propre: 'you are a one-part actress, and that one not a real part: you are an owl, sickened by two days of my sunshine'. But they remained friends and their true consummation was her performance of Eliza.

The success and fame of *Pygmalion* were assured on the opening night by the scandal caused when Mrs Pat delivered the notorious line, 'Not bloody likely,' at the end of Eliza's first public outing. Shaw's biographer Michael

Holroyd describes the reaction: 'The audience gave a gasp, there was a crash of laughter while Mrs Pat perambulated the stage, and then a second burst of laughing. The pandemonium lasted well over a minute.' The publicity was invaluable, and the play ran for months.

Given the success of *Pygmalion*, it was inevitable that demands for a movie should follow. Shaw awaited the coming of sound in 1929. There was a disastrous German version in 1934. But then the maverick Hungarian film producer Gabriel Pascal showed up, and he and Shaw began a formidable partnership.

The film *Pygmalion*, co-directed by Anthony Asquith and Leslie Howard, was critically and commercially successful when released in 1938. It went on to win two Oscars: one for Shaw's screenplay, the other for Wendy Hiller as Best Actress. A stage actress up to that point, Hiller would, Shaw predicted, be 'the film sensation of the next five years'. He wasn't far wrong.

He was a good deal less happy with the casting of Leslie Howard as Higgins, thinking he played the role in too romantic a manner. Shaw repeatedly attempted to damp down suggestions that Higgins and Eliza were romantically destined for each other; but actors and audiences always worked to prove the opposite, and generally prevailed.

In 1956, the afterlife of *Pygmalion* entered its final and most extraordinary phase. Shaw's play was turned into a stage musical, *My Fair Lady*, with fifteen songs written by Frederick Loewe with lyrics by Alan J Lerner. Many of those songs were memorable and fully in the spirit of Shaw's original, such as 'Wouldn't It Be Loverly', 'I Could Have Danced All Night', 'Why Can't the English' and 'I'm Getting Married in the Morning'. A twenty-one-year-old ingénue named Julie Andrews played Eliza, and made her reputation.

Higgins was impeccably rendered by Rex Harrison, who half-spoke, half-sang his lines. Harrison also played Higgins in the 1964 movie of *My Fair Lady* and won an Oscar for Best Actor. The movie Eliza was radiantly played by Audrey Hepburn, but she could not sing and so her voice was dubbed by Marni Nixon.

Shaw had resisted efforts during his lifetime to turn *Pygmalion* into a musical, insisting that the play had 'its own verbal music'. Notwithstanding, the appeal of *My Fair Lady* has proved enduring and the joint success of play, movie and musical render this Shaw's best-loved work.

FROM
PYGMALION

FROM ACT ONE

[Covent Garden]

THE FLOWER GIRL [*with feeble defiance*] I've a right to
be here if I like, same as you.

THE NOTE TAKER. A woman who utters such
depressing and disgusting sounds has no right to be
anywhere – no right to live. Remember that you are a
human being with a soul and the divine gift of articu-
late speech: that your native language is the language
of Shakespeare and Milton and the Bible; and don't
sit there crooning like a bilious pigeon.

THE FLOWER GIRL [*quite overwhelmed, looking up at
him in mingled wonder and deprecation without daring
to raise her head*] Ah-ah-ah-ow-ow-ow-oo!

THE NOTE TAKER [*whipping out his book*] Heavens!
What a sound! [*He writes; then holds out the book and reads,
reproducing her vowels exactly*] Ah-ah-ah-ow-ow-ow-oo!

THE FLOWER GIRL [*tickled by the performance, and
laughing in spite of herself*] Garn!

THE NOTE TAKER. You see this creature with her kerb-stone English: the English that will keep her in the gutter to the end of her days. Well, sir, in three months, I could pass that girl off as a duchess at an ambassador's garden party. I could even get her a place as lady's maid or shop assistant, which requires better English.

FROM ACT THREE

[Mrs Higgins's drawing-room]

[Eliza, who is exquisitely dressed, produces an impression of such remarkable distinction and beauty as she enters that they all rise, quite fluttered. Guided by Higgins's signals, she comes to Mrs Higgins with studied grace.]

ELIZA [*speaking with pedantic correctness of pronunciation and great beauty of tone*] How do you do, Mrs Higgins? [*She gasps slightly in making sure of the H in Higgins, but is quite successful*] Mr Higgins told me I might come.

MRS HIGGINS [*cordially*] Quite right. I'm very glad indeed to see you. [...]

[A long and painful pause ensues]

MRS HIGGINS [*at last, conversationally*] Will it rain, do you think?

ELIZA. The shallow depression in the west of these islands is likely to move slowly in an easterly direction.

There are no indications of any great change in the barometrical situation.

FREDDY. Ha! Ha! How awfully funny!

ELIZA. What is wrong with that, young man? I bet I got it right.

FREDDY. Killing!

MRS EYNSFORD HILL. I'm sure I hope it won't turn cold. There's so much influenza about. It runs right through our whole family regularly every spring.

ELIZA [*darkly*] My aunt died of influenza: so they said.

MRS EYNSFORD HILL [*clicks her tongue sympathetically*] !!!

ELIZA [*in the same tragic tone*] But it's my belief they done the old woman in.

MRS HIGGINS [*puzzled*] Done her in?

ELIZA. Ye-e-e-es, Lord love you! Why should she die of influenza? She come through diptheria right enough the year before. I saw her with my own eyes. Fairly blue with it, she was. They all thought she was dead; but my father he kept ladling gin down her throat till she came to so sudden that she bit the bowl off the spoon.

MRS EYNSFORD HILL [*startled*] Dear me!

ELIZA [*piling up the indictment*] What call would a woman with that strength in her have to die of influenza? What become of her new straw hat that should have come to me? Somebody pinched it; and what I say is, them as pinched it done her in.

MRS EYNSFORD HILL. What does doing her in mean?

HIGGINS [*hastily*] Oh, that's the new small talk. To do a person in means to kill them.

MRS EYNSFORD HILL [*to Eliza, horrified*] You surely don't believe that your aunt was killed?

ELIZA. Do I not! Them she lived with would have killed her for a hat-pin, let alone a hat.

MRS EYNSFORD HILL. But it can't have been right for your father to pour spirits down her throat like that. It might have killed her.

ELIZA. Not her. Gin was mother's milk to her. Besides, he'd poured so much down his own throat that he knew the good of it.

MRS EYNSFORD HILL. Do you mean that he drank?

ELIZA. Drank! My word! Something chronic. [...]

HIGGINS [*rising and looking at his watch*] Ahem!

ELIZA [*looking round at him; taking the hint; and rising*] Well: I must go. [...] Goodbye, all.

FREDDY [*opening the door for her*] Are you walking across the Park, Miss Doolittle? If so –

ELIZA [*with perfectly elegant diction*] Walk! Not bloody likely! [*Sensation*] I am going in a taxi. [*She goes out*] [...]

HIGGINS [*eagerly*] Well? Is Eliza presentable [*he swoops on his mother and drags her to the ottoman, where she sits down in Eliza's place with her son on her left*]?

[*Pickering returns to his chair on her right.*]

MRS HIGGINS. You silly boy, of course she's not presentable. She's a triumph of your art and of her dressmaker's; but if you suppose for a moment that she doesn't give herself away in every sentence she utters, you must be perfectly cracked about her.

FROM ACT FOUR

[*The Wimpole Street Laboratory*]

HIGGINS. What the devil have I done with my slippers?

[*He appears at the door*]

ELIZA [*snatching up the slippers and hurling them at him one after the other with all her force*] There are your slippers. And there. Take your slippers; and may you never have a day's luck with them!

HIGGINS [*astounded*] What on earth – ? [*He comes to her*] What's the matter? Get up. [*He pulls her up*] Anything wrong?

ELIZA [*breathless*] Nothing wrong – with you. I've won your bet for you, haven't I? That's enough for you. *I* don't matter, I suppose.

HIGGINS. You won my bet! You! Presumptuous insect! *I* won it. What did you throw those slippers at me for?

ELIZA. Because I wanted to smash your face. I'd like to kill you, you selfish brute. Why didn't you leave me where you picked me out of – in the gutter? You thank God it's all over, and that now you can throw me back again there, do you? [*She crisps her fingers frantically*]

HIGGINS [*looking at her in cool wonder*] The creature is nervous, after all.

ELIZA [*gives a suffocated scream of fury, and instinctively darts her nails at his face*] !!

HIGGINS [*catching her wrists*] Ah, would you? Claws in, you cat. How dare you show your temper to me? Sit down and be quiet. [*He throws her roughly into the easy-chair*]

ELIZA [*crushed by superior strength and weight*] What's to become of me? What's to become of me?

HIGGINS. How the devil do I know what's to become of you? What does it matter what becomes of you?

ELIZA. You don't care. I know you don't care. You wouldn't care if I was dead. I'm nothing to you – not so much as them slippers.

HIGGINS [*thundering*] Those slippers!

ELIZA [*with bitter submission*] Those slippers. I didn't think it made any difference now.

Shaw strikes a combative pose outside his revolving shed, where he wrote: words were his weapons.

CHAPTER FIVE

THE
FIRST
WORLD WAR
AND
EASTER
1916

COMMON SENSE ABOUT THE WAR

(1914)

The First World War broke out on 28 July 1914. In November, a mere four months later, Shaw's eighty-page treatise *Common Sense About the War* was published as a supplement in *The New Statesman*. Shaw's particular targets were the patriotism and jingoism prevalent in the early stages of the war: the conflict, he argued, should not be read as a melodramatic encounter between the virtuous British soldier and the fiendish Hun, but as the almost inevitable clash of two powerful, aggressive countries.

Whatever about his diagnosis of the forces operating in World War One and its causes, Shaw proved most accurate when he waxed prophetic: he recognised that America would join the war and that the Allies would defeat Germany. But he warned the British to be generous in victory, lest exacting a severe punishment on the defeated enemy would lead in time to another war.

Shaw makes clear at the outset that he is writing as an Irishman, not as an Englishman. His Irishness was explicit and to the fore in all of his writings about World

War One. This, he claimed, gave him a non-partisan, 'many-sided' view of the war, rather than the determinedly single-minded view of the British patriot. He also declared that the views he expressed would most likely result in his being lynched.

This rhetorical flourish proved nearer the truth than he might have supposed, as *Common Sense About the War* unleashed a wave of hostility towards Shaw in England that took a long time to dissipate. His popularity in the theatre had been riding high with the success of *Pygmalion* earlier in the year; within months, no Shaw play was being staged in any London theatre. However, none of this hostile opposition prevented him from continuing to write as prolifically and controversially as ever during the four long years of the First World War.

FROM
COMMON SENSE ABOUT
THE WAR

The time has now come to pluck up courage and begin
to talk and write soberly about the war. At first the mere
horror of it stunned the more thoughtful of us; and even
now only those who are not in actual contact with or
bereaved relation to its heartbreaking wreckage can think
sanely about it, or endure to hear others discuss it coolly.
As to the thoughtless, well, not for a moment dare I suggest that for the first few weeks they were all scared out
of their wits; for I know too well that the British civilian does not allow his perfect courage to be questioned:
only experienced soldiers and foreigners are allowed the
infirmity of fear. But they certainly were – shall I say a
little upset? They felt in that solemn hour that England
was lost if only one single traitor in their midst let slip
the truth about anything in the universe. It was a per-
ilous time for me. I do not hold my tongue easily; and
my inborn dramatic faculty and professional habit as a
playwright prevent me from taking a one-sided view

even when the most probable result of taking a many-sided one is prompt lynching. Besides, until Home Rule emerges from its present suspended animation, I shall retain my Irish capacity for criticising England with something of the detachment of a foreigner, and perhaps with a slightly malicious taste for taking the conceit out of her. Lord Kitchener made a mistake the other day in rebuking the Irish volunteers for not rallying faster to the defence of 'their country'. They do not regard it as their country yet. He should have asked them to come forward as usual and help poor old England through a stiff fight. Then it would have been all right.

[...]

Let us have no more nonsense about the Prussian Wolf and the British Lamb, the Prussian Machiavelli and the English Evangelist. We cannot shout for years that we are boys of the bulldog breed, and then suddenly pose as gazelles. No. When Europe and America come to settle the treaty that will end this business (for America is concerned in it as much as we are) they will not deal with us as the lovable and innocent victims of a treacherous tyrant and a savage soldiery. They will have to consider how these two incorrigibly pugnacious and inveterately snobbish peoples, who have snarled at one another for forty years with bristling hair and grinning fangs, and are now rolling over with their teeth in one another's throats, are to be tamed into trusty watchdogs of the peace of the world. I am sorry to spoil the saintly image with a halo which the British Jingo journalist sees just now when he looks in the glass; but it must be done if we are to behave reasonably in the imminent day of reckoning.

[...]

Please let us hear no more of kicking your enemy when he is down so that he may be unable to rise for a whole century. We may be unable to resist the temptation to loot Germany more or less if we conquer her. We are already actively engaged in piracy against her, stealing her ships and selling them in our prize courts, instead of honestly detaining them until the war is over and keeping a strict account for them. When gentlemen rise in the House of Commons and say that they owe Germans money and do not intend to pay it, one must face the fact that there will be a strong popular demand for plunder. War, after all, is simply a letting loose of organised murder, theft and piracy on a foe; and I have no doubt the average Englishman will say to me what Falstaff said to Pistol concerning his share in the price of the stolen fan: 'Reason, you rogue, reason: do you think I'll endanger my soul *gratis*?' To which I reply, 'If you can't resist the booty, take it frankly, and know yourself for half patriot, half brigand; but don't talk nonsense about disablement. Cromwell tried it in Ireland. He had better have tried Home Rule. And what Cromwell could not do to Ireland we cannot do to Germany.'

O'FLAHERTY VC

(1915, 1920)

In 1915, Shaw wrote his second play specifically for the Abbey Theatre. When Sir Matthew Nathan, Under-Secretary for Ireland, asked Shaw for a play to help with recruitment, the latter produced *O'Flaherty VC*. The play was hardly an advertisement for recruitment to the war effort. It clearly demonstrated that Private Dennis ('Dinny') O'Flaherty had become less provincial in outlook through exposure to the wider world and his experience of the trenches. But the Western Front also persuaded him to declare: 'No war is right and all the holy water that Father Quinlan ever blessed couldn't make one right.'

O'Flaherty VC was not ultimately staged at the Abbey, in 1915 or thereafter. Nathan and General Sir John French, Commander-in-Chief of Home Forces, wrote to Yeats that any performance of the play in the current climate and on the vexed issue of conscription in Ireland would, they feared, lead to riots.

Lady Gregory was with the Abbey players in the US at this time; had she been there, one feels she would have supported Shaw and his play. Yeats, left on his own, caved in and the scheduled production did not proceed.

In 1917, Shaw attended a dress rehearsal of *O'Flaherty VC* by officers of the Royal Flying Corps in Treizennes in Belgium. The leading part was played by the former actor Robert Loraine and O'Flaherty's feisty girlfriend by Robert Gregory, Lady Gregory's son. This Irish airman was to meet his death less than a year later, when his plane crashed on the way back from a mission in Italy, as Yeats's memorable poem recounts.

FROM
O'FLAHERTY V.C.

SIR PEARCE MADIGAN. Does patriotism mean nothing to you?

DENIS O'FLAHERTY. It means different to me than

what it would to you, sir. It means England and England's king to you. To me and the like of me, it means talking about the English just the way the English papers talk about the Boshes. And what good has it ever done here in Ireland? It's kept me ignorant because it filled up my mother's mind, and she thought it ought to fill up mine too. It's kept Ireland poor, because instead of trying to better ourselves we thought we was the fine fellows of patriots when we were speaking evil of Englishmen that was as poor as ourselves and maybe as good as ourselves. The Boshes I kilt was more knowledgeable men than me: and what better am I now that I've kilt them? What better is anybody?

SIR PEARCE [*huffed, turning a cold shoulder to him*] I am sorry the terrible experience of this war – the greatest war ever fought – has taught you no better, O'Flaherty.

O'FLAHERTY [*preserving his dignity*] I don't know about its being a great war, sir. It's a big war; but that's not the same thing. Father Quinlan's new church is a big church: you might take the little old chapel out of the middle of it and not miss it. But my mother says there was more true religion in the old chapel. And the war has taught me that maybe she was right.

SIR PEARCE [*grunts sulkily*] !!

O'FLAHERTY [*respectfully but doggedly*] And there's another thing it's taught me too, sir, that concerns you and me, if I may make bold to tell it to you.

SIR PEARCE [*still sulkily*] I hope it's nothing you oughtn't to say to me, O'Flaherty.

O'FLAHERTY. It's this, sir: that I'm able to sit here now and talk to you without humbugging you; and that's what not one of your tenants or your tenants' childer ever did to you before in all your long life. It's a true respect I'm showing you at last, sir. Maybe you'd rather have me humbug you and tell you lies as I used, just as the boys here, God help them, would rather have me tell them how I fought the Kaiser, that all the world knows I never saw in my life, than tell them the truth. But I can't take advantage of you the way I used, not even if I seem to be wanting in respect to you and cocked up by winning the Cross.

SIR PEARCE [*touched*] Not at all, O'Flaherty. Not at all.

O'FLAHERTY. Sure what's the Cross to me, barring the little pension it carries? Do you think I don't know that there's hundreds of men as brave as me that never had the luck to get anything for their bravery but a curse from the sergeant, and the blame for the faults of them that ought to have been their betters? I've learnt more than you'd think, sir; for how would a gentleman like you know what a poor ignorant conceited creature I was when I went from here into the wide world as a soldier? What use is all the lying, and pretending, and humbugging, and letting on, when the day comes to you that your comrade is killed in the trench beside you, and you don't as much as look round at him until you trip over his poor body, and then all you say is to ask why the hell the stretcher-bearers don't take it out of the way. Why should I read the papers to be humbugged and lied to by them that had the cunning to stay at home and send me to fight for them? Don't talk to me or to any soldier of the war being right. No war is right; and all the holy water that Father Quinlan ever blessed couldn't make one right. There, sir! Now you know what O'Flaherty V.C. thinks; and you're wiser so than the others that only knows what he done.

HEARTBREAK HOUSE

(1916–1921)

Shaw wrote the play *Heartbreak House* during World War One, between March 1916 and May 1917. Developments in technology had seen the arrival of the

German Zeppelin over the English countryside in 1915 and the random throwing of bombs on largely civilian victims. This signalled a major change in the nature of modern warfare: extending its reach from the Front in France into England. Civilians were now vulnerable to being attacked and killed, women as well as men, and there were (thus far) no means of retaliating.

Initially, the dropping of bombs created a kind of exhilaration, as Shaw reported when describing a bombing raid around the area of Ayot St Lawrence in the English countryside, where he and Charlotte now lived: 'What is hardly credible, but true, is that the sound of the Zepp's engines was so fine, and its voyage through the stars so enchanting, that I positively caught myself hoping next night that there would be another raid.'

This mood of excitement is reproduced when the bombs fall at the close of *Heartbreak House*. Shaw extends this feeling to all but two of the characters in the play: the two predatory capitalists who seek safety in the gravel pit and are blown to bits. The inhabitants of Heartbreak House, and the newcomer Ellie Dunn in particular, welcome the arrival of the bombers and hope they will come again. It brings to an end the characters' bored and purposeless lives as, in Shaw's words, 'cultured, leisured Europe before the war'.

Heartbreak House was published in 1919, and first produced in New York in November 1920; and in London in November 1921. Shaw was charged with trotting out the same old bag of dramatic tricks and creating nothing new. But as the 1920s unfolded, with T.S. Eliot's *The Waste Land* and James Joyce's *Ulysses* in 1922 alone, *Heartbreak House* took its place among them as Shaw's great modernist masterpiece, with its radical disjunctions of mood and character, its dream-like atmosphere, its group of stranded characters and its apocalyptic ending.

FROM
HEARTBREAK HOUSE

[*A terrific explosion shakes the earth. They reel back into their seats, or clutch the nearest support. They hear the falling of the shattered glass from the windows*]

MAZZINI. Is anyone hurt?

HECTOR. Where did it fall?

NURSE GUINNESS [*in hideous triumph*] Right in the gravel pit: I seen it. Serve un right. I seen it. [*she runs away towards the gravel pit, laughing harshly*]

HECTOR. One husband gone.

CAPTAIN SHOTOVER. Thirty pounds of good dynamite wasted.

MAZZINI. Oh, poor Mangan!

HECTOR. Are you immortal that you need pity him? Our turn next.

[*They wait in silence and intense expectation. Hesione and Ellie hold each other's hand tight.*

A distant explosion is heard]

MRS HUSHABYE [*relaxing her grip*] Oh! They have passed us.

LADY UTTERWORD. The danger is over, Randall. Go to bed.

CAPTAIN SHOTOVER. Turn in, all hands. The ship is safe. [*He sits down and goes asleep*]

ELLIE [*disappointedly*] Safe!

HECTOR [*disgustedly*] Yes, safe. And how damnably dull the world has become again suddenly! [*He sits down*]

MAZZINI [*sitting down*] I was quite wrong, after all. It is we who have survived; and Mangan and the burglar –

HECTOR. – the two burglars –

LADY UTTERWORD. – the two practical men of business –

MAZZINI. – both gone. And the poor clergyman will have to get a new house.

MRS HUSHABYE. But what a glorious experience! I
hope they'll come again tomorrow night.

ELLIE [*radiant at the prospect*] Oh, I hope so.

[*Randall at last succeeds in keeping the home fires burning
on his flute.*]

'A DISCARDED DEFENCE
OF ROGER CASEMENT'

(1916)

With the execution of the Irish leaders after the
Rising of Easter 1916, Shaw nailed his colours as an
Irishman to the mast. He recognised sooner than most
that, by executing fourteen men, the British authorities
had made political martyrs of them: 'It is absolutely
impossible to slaughter a man in this position without
making him a martyr and a hero, even though the day
before the rising he may have been only a minor poet.'
The execution of the 1916 leaders ensured that the
Rising would continue to influence developments in
Ireland and between Ireland and England long after the
short-term failure.

It was too late to help the executed leaders. But Shaw saw his opportunity to intervene a few months later with the trial in London of Sir Roger Casement for the capital crime of treason. Shaw wrote an audacious speech for Casement to deliver from the dock.

In a classically Shavian turn, Casement does not seek to deny the charge: he agrees that he had been trying to run German guns into Ireland to help with the planned uprising. But he turns the argument around by saying that he did not do so as an Englishman, but as an Irishman. This being the case, Shaw's argument ran that Casement should have been treated as a prisoner-of-war.

His dramatic monologue for Roger Casement is in the grand tradition of speeches from the dock of Irish rebels after they had been sentenced to death. But in a characteristic twist, the speech Shaw wrote for Casement was to be delivered before, not after, the verdict. Its aim was to prevent the prisoner from becoming a political martyr and to have him released back into a relatively anonymous civilian life.

Through a third party, Casement communicated his pleasure to Shaw about what the latter had written: 'I shall be so grateful if you will convey to Bernard Shaw my warmest thanks; his view is mine, with this exception – that I should never suggest to an English court or jury that they should let me off as a prisoner of war, but tell them "You may hang me, and be damned to you".'

In the event, Casement was persuaded by friends and counsel not to deliver Shaw's monologue; instead, he gave a more conventional speech after sentencing, which drew on some of Shaw's remarks. As Michael Holroyd writes in his biography of Shaw: 'Casement later regretted not using what he called "the only defence possible, viz., my own plan and that of G.B.S.".'

He was found guilty and sentenced to death. On 3 August 1916, Sir Roger Casement was hanged in Pentonville Prison. His remains would be returned to Dublin fifty years later.

FROM
'A DISCARDED DEFENCE
OF ROGER CASEMENT'

ROGER CASEMENT. Almost all the disasters and difficulties that have made the relations of Ireland with England so mischievous to both countries have arisen from the failure of England to understand that Ireland is not a province of England but a nation, and to negotiate with her on that assumption. If you persist in treating me as an Englishman, you bind yourself thereby to hang me as a traitor before the eyes of the world. Now as a simple matter of fact, I am neither an Englishman nor a traitor: I am an Irishman, captured in a fair attempt to achieve the independence of my country; and you can no more deprive me of the honours of that position, or destroy the effects of my effort, than the abominable cruelties inflicted six hundred years ago on William Wallace in this city [London], when he met a precisely similar indictment with a precisely similar reply, have prevented that brave and honorable Scot from becoming the national hero of his country. It may seem to some of you gentlemen of the jury that if I ought not to be hanged for being a patriot, I ought to be hanged for being a fool. I will not plead that if men are to be hanged for errors of judgement in politics, we should have such a mortality in England and Ireland that hardly one of us would be left to hang the other. But I may ask you if you nevertheless lean to that opinion in my case, whether my attempt, desperate as it seems, has been after all so disastrous a failure. I am not trying to shirk the British scaffold: it is the altar on which the Irish saints have been canonised for centuries; but I confess I shrink a little from the pillory in which the public opinion of the world places men who, with the best intentions, can do nothing but mischief to the cause they embrace. But I do not think I shall occupy that pillory. Will you understand me when I say that those three days of splendid fighting against desperate odds in the streets of Dublin have given back Ireland her self-respect? We were beaten, indeed never had a dog's chance of victory; but you also were beaten in a no less rash and desperate enterprise in Gallipoli. Are you ashamed of it? Did your hearts burn any the less – did your faith in the valour of your race flag and falter because you were at last driven into the sea by the Turks? Well, what you feel about the fight in Gallipoli, Irishmen feel all over the world about the fight in Dublin. Even if it had had no further consequences – even if it had not sent your Prime Minister, who shelved the Home Rule Act as if it had been a negligible parish by-law, scuttling to Dublin and forced *The Times* to say at last that Dublin Castle is no longer possible, I should still glory in that feat of arms.

And now, gentlemen, you may hang me if you like ...

Shaw striding purposefully into the future: he lived to the age of ninety-four.

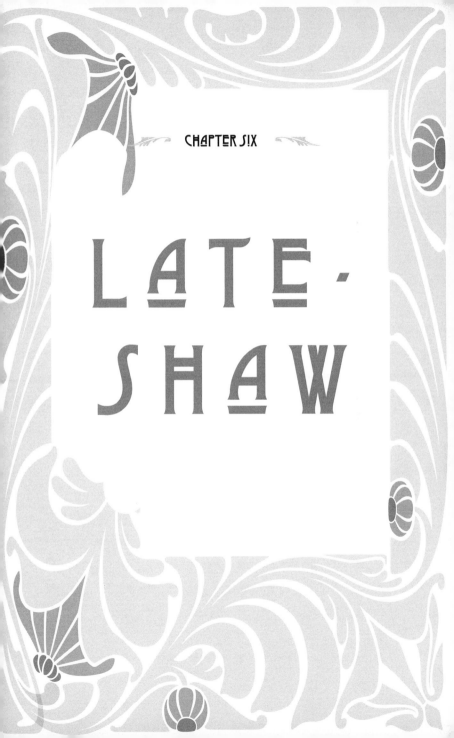

CHAPTER SIX

LATE-
SHAW

SANCTITY,
MULTICULTURALISM AND
DICTATORS
ST JOAN

(1923)

On 16 May 1920, the Vatican announced the canonisation of Joan of Arc, almost 500 years after she was burned at the stake. Shaw had long been interested in writing a dramatic version of the young Frenchwoman's life, her trial, martyrdom and reputation. Joan's canonisation provided the spark.

The writing went quickly: the words 'came tumbling out at such speed that my pen rushed across the paper'. The arguments in the play had a force and complexity that was rare even by Shaw's standards: he was determined not to turn Archbishop Cauchon and the Inquisitor into bad guys.

Joan emerges as the voice of individual conscience speaking out in defence of her freedom. In resisting the authority of the Church and following the promptings of her inner voices, Joan is presented by Shaw as the first Protestant. Bringing all of the French regions into a single force to expel the occupying English, she is also an early nationalist: 'God made them just like us; but he gave them their own country and their own language; and it is not His will that they should come into our country and try to speak our language.'

Among those impressed by Shaw's *St Joan* was the committee in charge of the Nobel Prize for Literature. Shaw had been considered and turned down several times before. He felt that *St Joan* had swung it for him, and wrote about the 'worrying odour of sanctity' that now seemed to emanate from him.

Shaw disliked the whole idea of literary prizes and declared that 'the Nobel Prize has been a hideous calamity for me, [...] really almost as bad as my seventieth birthday'. He accepted the prize, however, with 'my best thanks', but turned down the considerable prize money. Instead he requested that it be used to translate Swedish authors into English.

FROM ST JOAN

SCENE SIX

JOAN [*rising in consternation and terrible anger*] Perpetual imprisonment! Am I not then to be set free?

LADVENU [*mildly shocked*] Set free, child, after such
    wickedness as yours! What are you dreaming of?

JOAN. Give me that writing. [*She rushes to the table;
    snatches up the paper; and tears it into fragments*] Light
    your fire: do you think I dread it as much as the life of
    a rat in a hole? My voices were right.

LADVENU. Joan! Joan!

JOAN. Yes: they told me you were fools [*the word gives
    great offence*], and that I was not to listen to your fine
    words nor trust to your charity. You promised me my
    life; but you lied [*indignant exclamations*]. You think
    that life is nothing but not being stone dead. It is not
    the bread and water I fear: I can live on bread: when
    have I asked for more? It is no hardship to drink water
    if the water be clean. Bread has no sorrow for me, and
    water no affliction. But to shut me from the light of the
    sky and the sight of the fields and flowers; to chain my
    feet so that I can never again ride with the soldiers nor
    climb the hills; to make me breathe foul damp darkness
    and keep me from everything that brings me back to
    the love of God when your wickedness and foolishness
    tempt me to hate Him; all this is worse than the fur-
    nace in the Bible that was heated seven times. I could
    do without my warhorse; I could drag about in a skirt; I
    could let the banners and the trumpets and the knights

and soldiers pass me and leave me behind as they leave the other women, if only I could still hear the wind in the trees, the larks in the sunshine, the young lambs crying through the healthy frost, and the blessed blessed church bells that send my angel voices floating to me on the wind. But without these things I cannot live; and by your wanting to take them away from me, or from any human creature, I know that your counsel is of the devil, and that mine is of God.

THE ASSESSORS [*in great commotion*] Blasphemy! Blasphemy! She is possessed. She said our counsel was of the devil. And hers of God. Monstrous! The devil is in our midst, etc., etc.

D'ESTIVET [*shouting above the din*] She is a relapsed heretic, obstinate, incorrigible, and altogether unworthy of the mercy we have shown her. I call for her excommunication.

THE CHAPLAIN [to THE EXECUTIONER] Light your fire, man. To the stake with her.

[...]

LADVENU. I took this cross from the church for her that she might see it to the last: she had only two sticks that she put into her bosom. When the fire crept round us, and she saw that if I held the cross before her I should be burnt myself, she warned me to get down and save myself.

My lord: a girl who could think of another's danger in such a moment was not inspired by the devil. When I had to snatch the cross from her sight, she looked up to heaven. And I do not believe that the heavens were empty. I firmly believe that her Saviour appeared to her then in His tenderest glory. She called to him and died. This is not the end for her, but the beginning.

[...]

Siobhán McKenna as St. Joan in San Siubhan, her translation into Irish of Shaw's play. Taibhdhearc na Gaillimhe, 1950.

THE EXECUTIONER *comes in by the door behind the judges' chairs; and* WARWICK, *returning, finds himself face to face with him.*

WARWICK. Well, fellow: who are you?

THE EXECUTIONER [*with dignity*] I am not addressed as fellow, my lord. I am the Master Executioner of Rouen: it is a highly skilled mystery. I am come to tell your lordship that your orders gave been obeyed.

WARWICK. I crave your pardon, Master Executioner; and I will see that you lose nothing by having no relics to sell. I have your word, have I, that nothing remains, not a bone, not a nail, not a hair?

THE EXECUTIONER. The heart would not burn, my lord; but everything that was left is at the bottom of the river. You have heard the last of her.

WARWICK [*with a wry smile, thinking of what Ladvenu said*] The last of her? Hm! I wonder!

THE MILLIONAIRESS

(1934)

For four years after *St Joan* and the Nobel Prize, Shaw wrote no new plays. He concentrated instead on writing

The Intelligent Woman's Guide to Socialism and Capitalism (see Chapter One for an extract). In 1928, Shaw resumed playwriting with *The Apple Cart* and followed it with a rapid succession of new plays: *Too True To Be Good* (1931), *Village Wooing* (1933), *On the Rocks* (1933), *The Simpleton of the Unexpected Isles* (1934) and *The Millionairess* (1934). They all display an admirable lightness of touch and an unimpaired comic gift from a playwright now well into his seventies. But the overt ambition and 'big' themes of *Heartbreak House* and *St Joan* had been left behind.

The American theatre critic Joseph Wood Krutch said these new Shaw plays were entertaining, but devoid of 'serious meaning'. The dramatist's response was rapid and typically robust. He replied that he did not wish his audience to be overly conscious of his more serious aims; and since what he was invariably doing was 'going further and further afield' into dramatically unexplored terrain, he thought it would take some time for this more serious purpose to emerge.

Nowhere is this more apparent than in 1934's *The Millionnairess*. Its form is a romantic comedy, but with the complications and radical updating typical of Shaw. Epifania is extremely wealthy, but is looking for a man to love her for herself alone, and not for her money; she is also already married, wishing to divorce a husband who for his part wants a more placid and less combative life partner. There is a plausible suitor if this were a conventional comedy. But the potential new husband on whom Epifania sets her sights is a doctor who works for the poor and is wedded to Science; a socialist (or Bolshevik, as Epifania calls him) to oppose her dedication to Capitalism. Doctor Adrian is not a white man, however, but an Egyptian who follows Allah.

The Anglo-Indian author Hanif Kureishi, author of *The Buddha of Suburbia*, was very taken as a child with Peter Sellers' performance as the doctor in the 1960 film of *The Millionairess*. The son of an Indian father and a white English mother, Kureishi writes: 'I must have seen this on television and I don't recall many people of colour appearing in the movies I saw at the cinema with my father. Not only is Dr Adrian a Muslim man of colour and voluntarily poor, he is cultured, educated and dedicated to helping the indigent and racially marginalised.'

Shaw's Epifania is not in the least fazed by the fact that the man whom she has selected as her new husband is an Egyptian and a Muslim (though both her very English husband and her lover are); and what converts the doctor to a more positive view of Epifania is the beating of her pulse, not the colour of her skin: 'The pulse beats still, slow, strong. You are a terrible woman; but I love your pulse. I have never felt anything like it before.'

What is now required is a production of *The Millionairess* with a mixed-race actor as the male lead, not a white man in black face – not even one as brilliant as Peter Sellers.

FROM
THE MILLIONAIRESS

ACT TWO

A serious looking middleaged Egyptian gentleman in an old black frock coat and a tarboosh, speaking English too well to be mistaken for a native, hurries in.

THE EGYPTIAN (*peremptorily*) What's the matter? What is going on here?

EPIFANIA (*raising her head slowly and gazing at him*) Who the devil are you?

THE EGYPTIAN. I am an Egyptian doctor. I hear a great disturbance. I hasten to ascertain the cause. I find you here in convulsions. Can I help?

EPIFANIA. I am dying.

THE DOCTOR. Nonsense! You can swear. The fit has subsided. You can sit up now: you are quite well. Good afternoon.

EPIFANIA. Stop. I am not quite well: I am on the point of death. I need a doctor. I am a rich woman.

THE DOCTOR. In that case you will have no difficulty in finding an English doctor. Is there anyone else who needs my help? I was upstairs. The noise was of somebody falling downstairs. He may have broken some bones. [*He goes out promptly.*]

EPIFANIA [*struggling to her feet and calling after him*] Never mind him [her lover, Adrian, whom she has just thrown downstairs because he has insulted her father]: if he has broken every bone in his body it is no more than he deserves. Come back instantly. I want you. Come back. Come back.

THE DOCTOR [*returning*] The landlord is taking the gentleman to the Cottage Hospital in your car.

EPIFANIA. In my car! I will not permit it. Let them get an ambulance.

THE DOCTOR. The car has gone. You should be very glad that it is being so useful.

EPIFANIA: It is your business to doctor me, not to lecture me.

THE DOCTOR: I am not your doctor: I am not in general practice. I keep a clinic for penniless Mahometan refugees; and I work in the hospital. I cannot attend to you.

EPIFANIA. You can attend to me. You must attend to me. Are you going to leave me here to die?

THE DOCTOR. You are not dying. Not yet, at least. Your own doctor will attend to you.

EPIFANIA. You are my own doctor. I tell you I am a rich woman: doctors' fees are nothing to me: charge me what you please. But you must and shall attend to me. You are abominably rude; but you inspire confidence as a doctor.

THE DOCTOR. If I attended all those in whom I inspire confidence I should be worn out in a week. I have to reserve myself for poor and useful people.

EPIFANIA. Then you are either a fool or a Bolshevik.

THE DOCTOR. I am nothing but a servant of Allah.

EPIFANIA. You are not: you are my doctor: do you hear? I am a sick woman: you cannot abandon me to die in this wretched place.

THE DOCTOR. I see no symptoms of any sickness about you. Are you in pain?

EPIFANIA. Yes. Horrible pain.

THE DOCTOR. Where?

EPIFANIA. Don't cross-examine me as if you didn't believe me. I must have sprained my wrist throwing that beast all over the place.

THE DOCTOR. Which hand?

EPIFANIA [*presenting a hand*] This.

THE DOCTOR [*taking her hand in a businesslike way,*

and pulling and turning the fingers and wrist] Nothing
whatever the matter.

EPIFANIA. How do you know? It's my hand, not yours.

THE DOCTOR. You would scream the house down if
your wrist were sprained. You are shamming. Lying.
Why? Is it to make yourself more interesting?

EPIFANIA: Make myself interesting! Man: I am interesting.

THE DOCTOR. Not in the least, medically. Are you
interesting in any other way?

EPIFANIA. I am the most interesting woman in England.
I am Epifania Ognisanti di Parerga.

THE DOCTOR. Never heard of her.

DICTATORS
GENEVA

(1936)

I f Shaw had been prophetic about how World War One
was to end, he showed his own increasing limitations all
too damagingly when it came to World War Two. Having
confidently predicted there would be no war, he admitted
in a letter to the New Statesman of 5 July 1941: 'I said
there would be no war. I was wrong.' But Shaw was only

one of many people in England in the late 1930s who hoped that peace would prevail and that the globe would be spared another world war.

What is more disturbing in Shaw's case is the extent to which he approved of dictators like Mussolini, Hitler and Stalin in the 1920s and 1930s. As Fintan O'Toole puts it: 'The great seer failed to see the true nature of fascism, Nazism and Stalinism; he wanted to believe that the total-itarian regimes of Mussolini, Hitler and Stalin were rough harbingers of real progress and true democracy.'

Shaw was flattered by visits to Italy and Russia where he was feted, wined and dined. In old age he would appear to have lost faith in the gradualist, consensual approach to social reform of the Fabians. Instead, he looked impatiently for exceptional leaders to impose order from above.

His view of Russia and Stalin was informed by his delight in seeing a socialist programme embodied in a whole society, so much so that he would turn a blind eye to its widespread murder of dissidents. But with regard to Mussolini and Hitler Shaw's endorsement was less abso-lute than is generally claimed. His praise of certain aspects of Mussolini's policy, such as his work to eliminate unem-ployment, was qualified by his perception of Mussolini as a ludicrous, bombastic figure out of melodrama.

In the Preface to his play *Geneva* (written after the war in 1945) Adolf Hitler is described as 'a born leader' who, increasingly drunk with power, turned into a 'mad Messiah': and Shaw was consistent in condemning anti-Semitism. *Geneva* (written in 1936, and much revised into the 1940s) is clearer than any of his polemical prose statements that Nazi policy with regard to the Jews is their extermination. In the play a number of European dictators are called before the League of Nations to answer charges from various individuals. These include thinly disguised versions of Hitler (Battler), Mussolini (Bombardone) and Franco (Flanco): these satiric portrayals of contemporary European dictators anticpate Charlie Chaplin's *The Great Dictator* three years later.

A Jewish character in *Geneva* warns in Act One that 'my oppressor [is] attempting to exterminate a section of the human race'; and Battler in Act IV manages no great defense of his policies when charged face to face. Shaw's play, as so often with drama, knows more and sees further than the limited perspective of the individual playwright.

FROM GENEVA

FROM ACT ONE

THE JEW. I have been assaulted, plundered, and driven from my native soil by its responsible ruler. I, as a ruined individual, can do nothing. But the League of Nations can act through its Committee for Intellectual Co-operation. The Committee can act through the permanent court of International Justice at the Hague, which is also an organ of the League. My business here is to ask the Committee to apply to the court for a warrant against the responsible ruler. I charge him with assault and battery, burglary –

SHE. Burglary! Did they break into your house?

THE JEW. I cannot speak of it. Everything I treasured. Wrecked! Smashed! Defiled! Never will I forgive: never can I forget.

SHE. But why didn't you call the police?

THE JEW. Mademoiselle: the police did it. The Government did it. The Dictator who controls the police is responsible before Europe! Before civilization! I look to the League of Nations for redress.

It alone can call unrighteous rulers to account. The initiative must be taken by its Committee for Intellectual Co-operation: that is, for the moment, by you, mademoiselle.

SHE. But what can I do? I can't go out and collar your unrighteous ruler.

THE JEW. No, mademoiselle. What you must do is to write to the International Court, calling on it to issue a warrant for the arrest of my oppressor on a charge of attempting to exterminate a section of the human race.

[...]

FROM ACT FOUR

BATTLER [Hitler]. Do I stand accused? Of what, pray?

THE JEW [*springing up*] Of murder. Of an attempt to exterminate the flower of the human race.

BATTLER. What do you mean?

THE JEW. I am a Jew.

BATTLER. Then what right have you in my country? I exclude you as the British exclude the Chinese in Australia, as the Americans exclude the Japanese in California.

JEW. Why do the British exclude the Chinese? Because the Chinaman is so industrious, so frugal, so trustworthy, that nobody will employ a white British workman or caretaker if there is a yellow one within reach.

Why do you exclude the Jew? Because you cannot
compete with his intelligence, his persistence, his fore-
sight, his grasp of finance. It is our talents, our virtues,
that you fear, not our vices.

BATTLER. And am I not excluded for my virtues? I may
not set foot in England until I declare that I will do
no work there and that I will return to my own country in a few weeks. In every country the foreigner is a
trespasser. On every coast he is confronted by officers
who say you shall not land without your passport, your
visa. If you are of a certain race or colour you shall not
land at all. Sooner than let German soldiers march
through Belgium England plunged into war. Every
State chooses its population and selects its blood. We
say that ours shall be Nordic, not Hittite: that is all.

JEW. A Jew is a human being. Has he not a right of way
and settlement everywhere upon the earth?

BATTLER. Nowhere without a passport. That is the law
of nations.

JEW. I have been beaten and robbed. Is that the law of
nations?

BATTLER. I am sorry. I cannot be everywhere. And all
my agents are not angels.

THE JEW [*triumphantly*] Ah! Then you are NOT God
Almighty, as you pretend to be. [*To the Judge*] Your

honor: I am satisfied. He has admitted his guilt. [*He flings himself back into his seat*].

BATTLER. Liar. No Jew is ever satisfied. Enough. You have your warning. Keep away; and you will be neither beaten nor robbed. Keep away, I tell you. The world is wide enough for both of us. My country is not.

THE JEW. I leave myself in the hands of the court. For my race there are no frontiers. Let those who set them justify themselves.

[...]

JUDGE. Your objective is domination: your weapons fire and poison, starvation and ruin, extermination by every means known to science. You have reduced one another to such a condition of terror that no atrocity makes you recoil and say that you will die rather than commit it. You call this patriotism, courage, glory. There are a thousand good things to be done in your countries. They remain undone for hundreds of years; but the fire and the poison are always up to date. If this be not scoundrelism what is scoundrelism? I give you up as hopeless. Man is a failure as a political animal. The creative forces which produce him must produce something better.

CODA

On 10 September 1950 Bernard Shaw fell out of a tree he was pruning in the garden at Ayot. He was ninety-four years of age and had enjoyed reasonably good health into his nineties. But the fall resulted in a fracture which led to further complications with kidney and bladder and he died on 2 November of that year.

The last decade of his life had seen only two full-length plays, neither of them major, and a succession of dramatic squibs, the last of them a commissioned puppet play, *Shakes Versus Shav*. His major artistic achievements in the 1940s were his screenplays for two more films, *Major Barbara* in 1941 and *Caesar and Cleopatra* in 1945/6. As with *Pygmalion*, Shaw opened up the play of *Major Barbara* successfully in a number of scenes, the most important of which shows her wandering by the river and considering suicide. The films benefited from Shaw's scripts and from outstanding performances. Wendy Hiller returned as Major Barbara partnered by a young Rex Harrison as Adolphus Cusins, well over a decade before his Henry Higgins on stage and film. Shaw's Cleopatra was played by Vivian Leigh, then the most beautiful woman in the world and an accomplished Oscar-winning actress. The problem with these 1940s films was that Gabriel Pascal, no longer content to act as producer, now wanted to direct. He was clearly less proficient at directing than producing, as the heavy handedness of the results demonstrated. *Major Barbara* was improved, however, by the Assistant Direction of one of its young technical staff who would go on to direct his own films later that year: David Lean. Lean's assured artistic touch is most apparent in the intimate scenes involving Wendy Hiller's sublime Barbara.

In 1946 Shaw was offered and happily accepted the Honorary Freedom of Dublin, claiming it made him its oldest living native. He remembered Ireland in his will, as did Charlotte. The three organisations nominated by Shaw to receive his accumulated funds and future earnings were: the Royal Academy of Dramatic Art, which was to train the actors of the future; the British Museum 'in acknowledgement of the incalculable value to me of my daily resort to the Reading Room of that Institution at the beginning of my career'; and reaching further back to the National Gallery of Ireland where a young anonymous Dubliner 'owe[d] much of the only real education I ever got as a boy in Éire'. With the Shaw bequest, Ireland's National Gallery was able to purchase numerous paintings, both

Irish and European, in the seven decades following the playwright's death. Those funds were considerably boosted by the success of *My Fair Lady* both on stage and film. Charlotte Shaw's will bequeathed the most of her funds to an Irish bank, which was then to disseminate them to various Irish associations 'having for its object the bringing of the masterpieces of fine art within the reach of the people of all classes in their own country'.

When an interviewer asked whether he would be buried in Irish soil, Shaw replied: 'My ashes will be mixed inseparably with those of my wife, which are being kept for that purpose; and when that is done, neither of us will concern ourselves with what happens to them afterwards.' He said he always preferred the garden to the cloister.

SOURCES

The extracts from Shaw's plays are taken from *The Bodley Head Bernard Shaw: Collected plays with their prefaces*, edited by Dan H. Laurence, 7 volumes (London: Bodley Head, 1970–74). The dates given for each of the plays refer to the year in which Shaw finished its composition. Shaw's idiosyncratic punctuation has been silently corrected: e.g. possessives have been added.

The extracts from Shaw's prose writings are taken from the following editions: *The Quintessence of Ibsenism* (New York: Hill and Wang, 1957);

What Shaw Really Wrote About the War, edited by J.L. Wisenthal and Daniel O'Leary (Gainesville: University Press of Florida, 2006); and *The Intelligent Woman's Guide to Socialism, Capitalism, Sovietism and Fascism*, foreword by Polly Toynbee (Richmond, Surrey: Alma Books, 2012).

The text of Shaw's 1911 lecture on socialism is taken from Allan Chappelow, *Shaw – 'The Chucker-Out': A biographical exposition and critique*, Foreword by Vera Brittain (London: George Allen and Unwin, 1969); the Roger Casement speech is from Bernard Shaw, *The Matter With Ireland*, edited by David H. Greene and Dan H. Laurence, Second Edition (Gainesville: The University Press of Florida, 2001).

Biographical details are taken from Michael Holroyd, *Bernard Shaw*, four volumes (London: Chatto and Windus, 1988–92). For the Irish background, I have also consulted John O'Donovan, *G.B. Shaw* (Dublin: Gill and Macmillan, 1983).

The following critical works on Shaw have been drawn upon in the preparation of this volume:

Clare, David, *Bernard Shaw's Irish Outlook* (Basingstoke: Palgrave Macmillan, 2016).

Gahan, Peter (editor), *Shaw and the Irish Literary Tradition*, SHAW 30 (University Park, Pennsylvania: The Pennsylvania State University Press, 2010).

Gahan, Peter, *Bernard Shaw and Beatrice Webb on Poverty and Equality in the Modern World 1905–1914* (Basingstoke: Palgrave Macmillan, 2017).

Grene, Nicholas, *Bernard Shaw: A Critical View* (Houndmills: Macmillan, 1984).

Innes, Christopher (editor), *The Cambridge Companion to George Bernard Shaw* (Cambridge: Cambridge University Press, 1998).

Kent, Brad (editor), *George Bernard Shaw in Context* (Cambridge: Cambridge University Press, 2015).

O'Ceallaigh Ritschel, Nelson, *Shaw, Synge, Connolly and the Socialist Provocation* (Gainesville: University Press of Florida, 2011).

O'Ceallaigh Ritschel, Nelson, *Bernard Shaw, W.T. Stead and the New Journalism* (Basingstoke: Palgrave Macmillan, 2017).

O'Toole, Fintan, *Judging Shaw: The radicalism of G.B.S.* (Dublin: Royal Irish Academy, 2017).

ACKNOWLEDGEMENTS

My greatest acknowledgements in the preparation of this volume are to Peter Gahan and Nelson O'Ceallaigh Ritschel, to whom this book is gratefully dedicated. Their friendship and encyclopedic knowledge of Shaw were equally available to me throughout. I would also like to thank the following for stimulating discussions about Shaw: Nicholas Grene, Brad Kent, Declan Kiberd, Audrey MacNamara, Frank McGuinness, Emer O'Kelly. I would like to thank my publisher Michael O'Brien for inviting me to edit this volume and for always saying the right thing at the right time. My editor at the O'Brien Press, Eoin O'Brien, eased the book's way to publication and Emma Byrne provided the wonderful designs. My love and a big 'thank you' to my wife Katy Hayes, son Merlin and daughter Lily for their interest in and positivity about the project.